A RECOVERY TOOLBOX FOR WELLBEING

in the Early Years

The Toolbox of Wellbeing Series

A Toolbox of Wellbeing: Helpful strategies & activities for children, teens, their carers & teachers

A Recovery Toolbox for Wellbeing in the Early Years: Nurturing & wellbeing activities for children aged 3–6

A Recovery Toolbox for Primary-Aged Children: Nurturing & wellbeing activities for children aged 7–11

A Recovery Toolbox for Wellbeing for Adolescents & Teenagers: Nurturing & wellbeing activities for young people aged 12–16

My Toolbox of Wellbeing Journal: Creative, inspiring activities & strategies

A RECOVERY TOOLBOX FOR WELLBEING in the Early Years

Nurturing & Wellbeing Activities for Children Aged 3–6

Tina Rae & Ali D'Amario

HINTON HOUSE Essentials

HINTON HOUSE

First published in 2021 by
Hinton House Publishers Ltd
T +44 (0)1280 822557 E info@hintonpublishers.com

www.hintonpublishers.com

British Library Cataloguing in Publication Data
A CIP catalogue record for this book is available from the British Library.

ISBN 978 1 912112 53 1

Printed and bound in the United Kingdom

Contents

Preface

> *Never has there been a time when knowing how to manage your own wellbeing and how to support our children in doing this has been so vital.*
>
> ***Tina Rae (2020)***

At the time of writing this series of books we are in the middle of a global pandemic and many researchers across the world are warning that this coronavirus pandemic could inflict long-lasting emotional trauma on an unprecedented global scale. They assert that it could leave millions wrestling with debilitating psychological disorders, while dashing hopes for a swift economic recovery. The COVID-19 crisis has combined mental health stressors that have been studied before in other disasters, but which have never been seen consolidated in one global crisis.

It has left millions without jobs, sent billions into isolation and forced nearly everyone on earth to grapple with the feeling that they or those they love are suddenly physically vulnerable. The nature of the disease means that there can be no certainty about when the worst will pass. Hundreds of thousands have been infected, thousands have died, the virus continues to spread, and a vaccine could be more than a year away for everyone on the planet.

The scale of this outbreak as a traumatic event is almost beyond our comprehension as, unlike previous disasters such as 9/11 or World War 2, during which the anxiety caused was limited by geography, there are now no boundaries. Trying to understand this is difficult when the available research on how humans cope with such events covers how humans cope with quarantine, mass disasters and ongoing stressors, but not with all three simultaneously.

The concern of governments around the world is also focused on financial recovery options and forecasts, but does not appear to factor in the psychological effects: emotionally scarred consumers are likely to spend less and save more, bringing about a kind of 'Great Depression mind-set'. It seems that the sense of vulnerability will be long lasting, in that anxiety and fear as a result of the virus could outlast the pandemic itself.

Those who are financially crippled by the crisis or who experience the loss of loved ones are also the most susceptible to enduring psychological trauma and those who already had mental health problems, such as addiction, are also at risk. They will clearly find it much harder to draw on their resilience in order to bounce back.

This most at-risk group also includes the front-line service personnel and essential workers for whom mental health disorders inflicted during this crisis could exceed the consequences of the virus itself. However, it is also evident that that even those who are not directly affected by the crisis are at risk for post-traumatic stress disorder. For example, after 9/11 it became evident that even people who were not directly exposed to trauma, but spent many hours in front of the television or looking at their smart phones, were at high risk for psychopathology, including PTSD, depression and anxiety.

So, more than ever before, we can see the need to provide the appropriate support at an individual and whole-systems level for all populations experiencing this mental trauma. We know that those who suffer from mental health disorders can be treated with therapeutic interventions and, in some cases, medication.

But we also need to emphasise the fact that there are steps that individuals can take – even while the crisis continues – that can curb its psychological toll, such as limiting exposure to television news and social media, connecting with others, developing effective thinking skills, looking after their diet and exercise regimes, practising grounding and using a range of strategies to self-regulate the nervous system.

What prompted us to write this series of books was our sense of the enormity of this whole situation, as well as our feelings of helplessness to change things and make a difference. In effect, we wanted to play the role that we believe is the duty of psychologists. We needed to feel that we could encourage others – particularly young people – to take back some level of control and achieve a sense of autonomy, and one way to do this was to create these publications.

Giving psychology away has always been our joint aim. We now, more than ever, need to share what we know and empower others to make use of the evidence-based tools that work – we can no longer be precious about this. We are not suggesting we all can become therapists, but we are making the argument that, given this current crisis, it is more vital than ever that we do all become more therapeutic and learn how to use the strategies that therapists know to be effective. Most of this is common sense in our view and not rocket science. As you read, you will see how easy it can be to begin to ground yourself, to challenge negative thinking, to self-soothe, to connect and to self-regulate with Mindfulness and tools from Positive Psychology.

We both live and breathe this stuff. It comes from the heart. So, if this helps you and your children begin to take back a little bit of control and manage this ongoing level of stress and trauma then our work will have been worthwhile.

Tina Rae & Ali D'Amario
August 2020

What have the early years children said?

I miss my friends ...

They make me feel really angry but I'm lucky I haven't had them. I hope they go away soon.

The worst thing is I can't at all see my friends because if I was at school I would be able to. The best bit is that I get to spend days with my family.

I don't like at home ...

Why can't we go to the park?

I feel funny in my tummy ...

Covid is bad because it makes people too sick.

The germs came from underground and they are bad.

I am angry ...

I wanted a birthday party but we aren't allowed so it made me sad.

We can't hug anymore ...

Is Granny sick?

Will we all die if we go out?

Not being able to play with my friends makes me sad but I love playing games with Daddy everyday.

About the Authors

Dr Ali D'Amario is an educational and child psychologist working for the Xavier Catholic Education Trust. Within her role, she leads a team of 'mental health champions', trains and supervises emotional literacy support assistants, delivers training and parent workshops, as well as working with children at a group and individual level.

She trained at the University of East London under the supervision of Dr Tina Rae, who she credits for instilling her with a passion for supporting the wellbeing of others through nurture, compassion and all things kind. She is proud to be on the editorial advisory board for NurtureUK's *International Journal of Nurture in Education* (IJNE), and is co-author, with Tina Rae, of *Philosophy for Children: The man in the moon* (2014).

@AliDamarioEP

Dr Tina Rae has more thirty years' experience working with children, adults and families in both clinical and educational contexts within local authorities and specialist educational services. She currently works as a consultant educational and child psychologist in a range of SEMH and mainstream contexts and for Compass Fostering as a consultant psychologist supporting foster carers, social workers and looked-after children. From 2010 to 2016 she was an academic and professional tutor for the Doctorate in Educational and Child Psychology at the University of East London. Tina is a registered member of the Health and Care Professions Council and a full member of the British Psychological Society. She is also a member of ENSEC (European Network for Social and Emotional Competence) and a former trustee of the Nurture Group Network (NGN) now NurtureUK.

Tina is an award-winning author of more than 100 titles on topics including wellbeing, attachment, emotional literacy, behavioural problems, anger and stress management, critical incidents, Cognitive Behavioural Therapy, motivational interviewing, solution-focused brief therapy, loss and bereavement in young people, youth offending and social skills development.

Among her most recent publications are *A Toolbox of Wellbeing* (2020), *The ASD Girls' Wellbeing Toolkit: An evidence-based intervention promoting mental, physical & emotional health* (2019; Winner of the BESA Education Resources Awards 2020 Education Book of Year), *The Essential Guide to Using CBT with Children & Young People* (2018), *Identifying & Supporting Children with Sensory Processing Difficulties* (2018), *Understanding & Preventing Self-Harm in Schools* (2017), *The Essential Guide to Using Mindfulness with Children & Young People* (2017), all from Hinton House Publishers.

Tina is a regular speaker at both national and international conferences and provides training courses and supervision for school-based staff in special and mainstream contexts and educational psychology services across the UK and internationally.

tinarae@hotmail.co.uk
@DrTinarae

Introduction

The Recovery Toolbox of Wellbeing is a series of three books aimed at nurturing post-traumatic growth with children and young people and can be regarded as a must-have series for providing much needed practical advice and support to protect mental health and wellbeing at a time of uncertainty and fear.

A recent survey undertaken by the charity Young Minds in March 2020 revealed that the current coronavirus pandemic is having a profound effect on young people with existing mental health conditions. Although they understood the need for the measures taken in response to the virus, the report says, this did not lessen the impact. Many of those who took part in the survey reported increased anxiety, problems with sleep, panic attacks or more frequent urges to self-harm.

The Co-SPACE study (Dodd, Westbrook & Lawrence, 2020), a piece of research aiming to track the mental health of pre-school children during the pandemic, found that whilst worries about the coronavirus specifically were rare, the children were most concerned about not being able to see their friends. Indeed, parents reported that 47 per cent of the children had no other children to play with at home. As a result, concerns about their child's wellbeing were amongst the top concerns of parents, alongside the stresses of work and screen time. The study revealed that many parents would welcome assistance with how to manage their child's emotions and methods to support them in coming out of isolation.

Focus on the Early years

This book therefore focuses on providing resources and strategies specifically for children aged 3 to 6 alongside advice for teachers/parents and carers as to how to support them to build resilience, self-esteem, social skills, effective thinking, manage anxiety and worries and the transition back into their early years settings.

OFSTED (2020) identified that many children have left Early years settings since the first national restrictions and have not returned. Almost all providers they surveyed said that the pandemic had significantly impacted the learning and development of children who had left and subsequently returned. They were particularly concerned about children's personal, social and emotional development.

Some children had returned less confident and more anxious. In some cases, children had also become less independent, for example returning to their setting using dummies or back in nappies having previously been toilet trained. However, providers reported that children who continued to attend their setting or who were well supported at home had made good progress in their learning. Most said they have put more emphasis on personal, social and emotional development because they felt that children's skills had regressed. Some providers said their curriculum had stayed mostly the same but with small adaptations, such as allowing extra time for children to settle in with additional adult support on a one-to-one basis. Many providers have also made changes to the resources and routines in their settings and most have increased their teaching of personal hygiene.

Why We Wrote this Book

It is this research and our own personal awareness of the impact of this traumatic and frightening context that has primarily prompted us to write this series of books.

We know that the impact upon all of us is significant and, for those who already have mental health issues, the ongoing sense of fear and anxiety is especially concerning. The sense of uncertainty and the transition to a new and insecure reality and ways of living will continue to impact on all of us – adults and children alike.

The need to understand the impact of such trauma on the whole community has never been more vital. Although young people in this survey were able to identify some of the factors that they found helpful in a time of trauma, we recognise that there will be an ongoing need for us all to develop and make use of trauma-informed approaches in the aftermath of this pandemic. Children will need to find and build upon their inner resources of resilience and adults will need to do likewise, as well as learning how to talk to their children about their fears in a therapeutic way that enables them to heal and to cope in their new reality.

The ongoing concern

We know that our children, particularly those who already have existing mental health issues, will have found the lockdown experiences particularly stressful and increased levels of anxiety will be the norm. However, it is probably also the case that every child will be experiencing higher levels of stress and anxiety at this time and that when they return to the school context there will be enormous emotional and psychological hurdles to overcome. The need to provide support for increased levels of anxiety and managing the transition to a 'new normal' will be ongoing.

Never has there been a time when knowing how to manage your own wellbeing and how to support our children in doing this has been so vital.

What is Emotional & Psychological Trauma?

Emotional and psychological trauma is the result of extraordinarily stressful events that shatter our sense of security, making us feel helpless in a dangerous world. Psychological trauma can leave us struggling with upsetting emotions, memories, and anxiety that does not seem to go away. It can also leave us feeling numb, disconnected, and unable to trust other people.

Traumatic experiences often involve a threat to life or safety, but any situation that leaves us feeling overwhelmed and isolated can result in trauma, even if it does not involve physical harm. It is not the objective circumstances that determine whether an event is traumatic, but our subjective emotional experience of the event. The more frightened and helpless we feel, the more likely we are to be traumatised. Repeatedly viewing traumatic images can overwhelm our nervous system and create traumatic stress. This is certainly true in terms of access to social media and news reporting regarding the current pandemic. We know that the increase in anxiety for many of us is directly linked to continual exposure to such material. However, whatever the cause of our trauma, and whether it happened years ago or yesterday, we can make healing changes and move forwards – even flourishing in the post-traumatic growth period that ensues.

Protecting the Mental Health of Children after Trauma

The effects of traumatic experiences on children are sobering, but not all children are affected in the same way, or to the same degree. Children and families possess competencies, psychological resources and resilience (often even in the face of significant trauma) that can protect them from long-term harm. Teaching children the skills of resilience and providing them with opportunities to bounce back and renew themselves in the face of adversity is a precious gift.

- **Be there**. Research on resilience in children demonstrates that an essential protective factor is the reliable presence of a positive, caring and protective parent, caregiver, or significant other (such as a teacher), who can help shield children against adverse experiences (Sroufe *et al.*, 2005).

- **Support them to challenge underlying beliefs and thoughts.** Negative and irrational beliefs and thoughts, such as, 'If I don't look perfect, no one will like me', or 'I can't cope with difficult or scary situations,' are significant factors in generating anxiety. Model and communicate effective ways to question and challenge anxiety-provoking thoughts and beliefs.

- **Support them to accept uncertainty.** Uncertainty is one thing that people worry about a lot because of the potential for negative outcomes. As it is impossible to eliminate uncertainty, you can assist children to be more accepting of uncertainty and ambiguity.

- **Be a role model.** If you can manage your own anxiety, children will see that it can be managed and incorporate your strategies into their own behaviours. Teaching parents to manage their own anxiety has been shown to be helpful in reducing their children's anxiety.

- **Be patient.** Sometimes the behaviours of anxious children may seem unreasonable to others. It is important to remember that an anxious child who cries or avoids situations is, in fact, responding instinctively to a perceived threat. Changing avoidant behaviours takes time and persistence.

- **Balance reassurance with new ideas.** When a child comes to you with something they are worried about, listen and understand what is happening. Explore with them what they could do to manage their fears.

- **Show children some simple relaxation techniques.** Deep breathing, progressive muscle relaxation and meditation can be helpful as a way of learning how to better manage physical anxiety symptoms. Generally, these techniques are only effective if practised consistently over several weeks

- **Encourage plenty of physical exercise and appropriate sleep.** When people are well-rested and relaxed, they will be in a better mental state to handle fears or worries.

- **Moderate the consumption of products high in sugar.** High sugar products increase levels of anxiety, because they cause energy levels to spike and then crash. This leaves a person feeling drained and less able to deal with negative thoughts.

- **Make time for things that the child enjoys and finds relaxing.** These could be simple things, such as playing or listening to music, reading books or going for walks.

- **Help them to face the things or situations they fear**. Learning to face their fears and reduce avoidance of feared objects and situations, is one of the most challenging parts of overcoming anxiety. Facing fears usually works best if it is undertaken gradually, a step at a time.

- **Encourage help-seeking when needed**. Make sure that children know there are people who can help if they find that they cannot handle a problem on their own. Knowing that they can call on others for support, if needed, will make them feel less anxious about what might happen in the future.

The need to be resilient yourself

We know that unregulated and stressed adults cannot effectively support and help children who are also unregulated and stressed. It is impossible.

We also know that the direct carers of children are most effective in helping them develop self-regulation. They can provide activities that support regulation and are also the most immediate role models for children. The emotional tone of a school or children's home is dramatically affected by the capacity of adults to regulate themselves. If adults respond to children's distress in a calm but engaged way, they demonstrate an alternative way of managing stress. When adults respond to difficulties by becoming dysregulated, they replicate the damaging environments that characterised children's earlier experiences.

Kolk (2003) described trauma as 'speechless terror' and traumatised children may be slow to develop speech or may struggle to find words to describe their trauma or their feelings. Trauma may also affect the capacity to process verbal information. Traumatised children can struggle to follow complex directions and may experience auditory selectivity, so that only part of a verbal communication is heard. Adults often interpret failure to obey directions or to respond to questions as wilful defiance and react punitively, rather than modifying their own communication to match the children's needs. So, once again, we need to be careful to ensure that our responses and the systems we put in place, both in the home and in school, ensure these factors are considered. We must respond appropriately to children and young people who have experienced trauma and who are currently living through the traumatic times of this pandemic. We need to create safety routines first and to also change our own expectations and behaviours.

To achieve this, we need to ensure that we know how to engage in effective self-care and how to manage our own stress and anxiety, whilst simultaneously understanding the need to respond in a truly trauma-informed way. This has never been more important when we know that children are all experiencing such a stressful social and educational context (See Appendix 5, 'Trauma Recovery Self-Care Tips').

The need to provide feelings of safety at home & in school

Looking at the sensory environments where children live and learn can help to create feelings of safety. Our brains develop by recognising novel stimuli that may potentially indicate danger, but, in order to manage the sensory bombardment we all experience, we quickly tune out familiar stimuli. Eventually we just do not notice sensory signals that are familiar to us, but which may be very frightening or arousing to children who are hyper-vigilant. Working alongside children, we may identify and eliminate sensory triggers that affect them negatively and build in sensory cues that are soothing or appropriately stimulating.

At times children's behaviour is considered difficult or controlling, for example, needing a light on throughout the night or being unable to sleep without music to fill the unbearable silence, but these may be attempts to feel safe. Helping children create a sensory environment that manages their traumatic responses and provides new experiences that evoke safety, allows them a sense of control over their distress that can build strength and resilience.

Traumatised children find change exceedingly difficult. Disruption of routines, even for a positive reason, can evoke panic in children. Clear stable routines are very comforting to children, particularly at times involving transition from one state to another, such as shifting from sleeping to wakefulness, or moving from one place to another, such as from home to school. Where change is anticipated it is important to explain the reasons and rehearse with children what will be different and how they will be supported. When unexpected disruption arises, adults should be alert to the likely impact on children and proactively intervene to help them remain calm.

This is not always easy in the context of a busy school and very often the level of nurture and additional consideration may cause difficulties for some adults who do not have the capacity to manage on a day to day basis. Therefore, additional training and support may well be needed. This will be particularly important when transitioning children and young people back into the school communities after the current pandemic. There will be many children who will find this traumatic and have countless questions, concerns and fears about this whole process.

The need for additional training & support

We know that understanding the impact of trauma requires both cognitive and emotional learning. This is best accomplished by linking information about trauma with practitioners' own experience of caring for or educating traumatised children. Rather than employing a simple didactic approach, it should include reflective space for participants to consider their own attachment and trauma histories, as well as those of the children they care for.

Golding (2013), for example, has created a training resource for foster carers and adoptive parents incorporating concepts from attachment and trauma theory with practice-based discussion. PACE, a parenting attitude characterised by **p**layfulness, **a**cceptance, **c**uriosity and **e**mpathy, is explored in depth and carers are encouraged to try this out between sessions. She also introduces the concept of 'mind-mindedness' to help carers understand the internal worlds of children and fill developmental gaps created by an early failure of attuned and mind-mindful parenting. As well as increasing carers' knowledge, the course aims to decrease their stress and thus contributes to the stability of placements.

Engaging with traumatised children in an open and connected way is itself stressful and difficult and there is always a risk that practitioners and carers will experience vicarious trauma. 'Blocked care' (Hughes & Baylin, 2013) is a concept that describes the neurological impact on adults of caring for children who are unable to engage in reciprocal relationships. Hughes and Baylin describe 'brain-based' parenting as a way of investing in reflective support that can avert dangers to both children and those who care for or educate them.

Knowledge and understanding of brain-based nurturing should now become a key element in school strategies and new ways of parenting if we are to successfully meet the needs of our children and young people as they recover from the trauma of this pandemic.

It is also now essential that school leaders provide mental health training for all staff to ensure that there is a coherent and evidence-based approach to meeting the increasingly complex needs of the school population. This is not an easy task, given current financial and logistical constraints, but there are many useful resources available that are cost effective and can provide staff with a knowledge base and sense of confidence in their ability to develop their skills in responding to, and working more therapeutically with, children and young people. The role of the mental health leads in schools will be key here in leading the development of appropriate training and making use of available evidence-based training resources, such as *The Wellbeing Toolkit for Mental Health Leads* (Rae *et al.*, 2020).

Communicating authentically is key

Children and young people need to feel validated, heard and safe and adults need more than ever to develop the skills of authentic listening and the ability to emotion coach children through the feelings and behaviours they will experience on a daily basis. These are essential skills and the process of using emotion coaching needs to permeate our thinking and responses, both as parents and carers (See Appendix 4, 'Emotion Coaching Information Sheet').

To help a child recover from trauma, it is important for adults to communicate openly. They need to let them know that it is normal to feel scared or upset, and to remember that children may also look to them for cues on how they should respond to trauma; therefore letting them see how we are dealing with our own symptoms in a positive way is vital.

How Children React to Emotional & Psychological Trauma

- **Regression.** Many children need to return to an earlier stage where they felt safer. Younger children may wet the bed or want a bottle; older children may fear being alone. It is important to be understanding, patient and comforting if our child responds in this way.

- **Thinking the event is their fault.** Children younger than 8 years of age tend to think that if something goes wrong, it must be their fault. Be sure that the child understands that they did not cause the event.

- **Sleep disorders.** Some children have difficulty falling asleep; others wake frequently or have troubling dreams. Giving a younger child a stuffed animal, soft blanket, or flashlight to take to bed can be helpful, alongside spending extra time together in the evening, doing quiet activities or reading. Patience is key here. It may take a while before a child can sleep through the night again.

- **Feeling helpless.** Being active in a campaign to prevent an event from happening again, writing thank-you letters to people who have helped, and caring for others can bring a sense of hope and control to everyone in the family.

To summarise the key points, the things we know about trauma:

- Children in care are likely to have experienced trauma, but not all children who have adverse experiences will be traumatised. Every child is unique and their responses to the same adversity will differ.

- Trauma can affect brain development. Many traumatised children function at an earlier developmental level than their chronological age suggests.

- Traumatised children may struggle to develop regulatory skills needed for learning and social relationships.

- Some children react powerfully to sensory triggers related to their trauma by becoming hyper-aroused or dissociating. These reactions often occur below the level of conscious awareness.

- If adults involved with traumatised children are unable to manage their own emotions, this can escalate children's distress.

- Effective help requires intervention that is congruent with neuroscience, developmentally relevant and relational.

- The key adults in helping children recover from trauma are their carers and teachers. They require relevant support and training to be most helpful to traumatised children.

- Post-traumatic growth and resilience is possible. Traumatised children need hope and adults involved with them must believe in a positive future for them.

Using the Recovery Toolbox

If we think about looking after our bodies and keeping fit and well, it is easy to see how we also need to look after what is happening in our heads – how we think, feel and react to what happens to us in life.

Having good mental health means that we are generally able to think, feel and react in ways that make us able to connect with other people and lead a healthy and generally happy life. Not being able to manage our emotional, psychological and social wellbeing can feel just as bad as a physical illness, or even worse.

We have written this book with the intention of providing children in the early years and their carers/teachers easy to understand and use tools and strategies to foster good mental health and to build the resilience needed to move on from trauma – including that of having to live with the continual fear of the current Coronavirus pandemic.

All the activities are self-explanatory and straightforward. Since the book is aimed at children no more than about 6-years-old, it is assumed that the adult facilitator will assist in filling in the activity sheets, in spite of the fact that the text is frequently addressed directly to the child. In these instances, the instructions can also be read aloud to the child as necessary. We have included additional information in the appendices to explain in more detail some key tools, such as Mindfulness or strategies from Cognitive Behavioural Therapy (CBT), where we think this might be needed.

However, the idea here is to make this all accessible to the non-specialist. We want people to be able to pick up this book and feel safe in making use of the ideas and know that this is all evidence-based and has been tried and tested with children and young people over many years. This is *not* a therapeutic handbook and certainly does not replace the role of the specialist therapeutic professional. This is a resource for the non-specialist who is seeking to better understand mental health issues and protective factors and who needs to support and nurture our anxious children and young people at a time of real crisis in both education and in the social context.

A final note of caution

If the psychological trauma symptoms *do not* ease up – or if they become even worse – and the individual finds that they are unable to move on from the event for a prolonged period of time, they may be experiencing post-traumatic stress disorder. While emotional trauma is a normal response to a disturbing event, it becomes PTSD when our nervous system gets 'stuck' and we remain in psychological shock, unable to make sense of what happened or process our emotions.

Working through trauma can be scary, painful, and potentially re-traumatising, so this healing work is best undertaken with the help of an experienced trauma specialist.

To seek additional help of this nature for a child (or an adult) it is clearly essential in the first instance to discuss with the GP and then to seek an appropriate referral. A list of specialist agencies and charities are included in the appendices to this book, which may also be helpful should you need to seek additional support.

1 Self-Regulation Activities

Self-regulation is the ability to understand and control your behaviour and your emotional reactions. This includes being able to calm yourself down when experiencing big emotions, such as anxiety, anger or excitement. Self-regulation skills also allow us to focus on the task at hand, and respond with socially appropriate behaviour, rather than showing how we might really feel. We develop these skills as we grow and our brains develop; hence, while a 2-year-old might throw themselves on the floor in the supermarket when they are bored, an older child or adult may respond differently to the same feelings. Self-regulation skills are important because they help children to control their impulses, maintain relationships with other children during play, and manage their stress levels. Through this self-regulation, they are able to feel safe, content, and able to learn.

Self-regulation skills start to develop in infancy. When children have experienced co-regulation through consistent, sensitive relationships, they begin to learn how to manage their own emotions. Neuroscientific research suggests that these relationships help to develop the links between the emotional limbic brain, and the cerebral cortex, allowing children to be better able to rationalise, reason, empathise and problem-solve. However, the cerebral cortex is not thought to be fully developed until the mid-twenties, and therefore children, adolescents and even adults need support with self-regulation at times. Due to their brain development, it is crucial to support a child to regulate their emotions before trying to reason with them.

Some calming techniques to teach young children to help them self-regulate include:

- Mindfulness
- Visualisation
- Grounding
- Sensory activities
- Controlled breathing

These techniques have been incorporated into the activities in this section, along with activities designed to help your children to identify their emotions. Research shows that labelling emotions can help to reduce the intensity of the emotion (Torre & Lieberman, 2018), and therefore teaching this skill is integral in allowing children to start to manage their own emotions.

Activity 1.1

Mindful Bubbles

If your child has something that is on their mind, try this activity to help them to bring their focus to the present moment and relax. Blow bubbles together and watch the bubbles as they float into the air.

Focus on the beautiful colours, the smell of the bubble liquid, watch them as they float away, and see if you can even hear them burst into tiny droplets.

Try to catch the bubbles on your arms, hands and face to see how they feel against your skin.

As you watch one of the bubbles, imagine putting your worry inside the bubble, and as you watch it float away and pop, feel the worries float away with it . . .

Reflection

What colours could you see in the bubbles?
What did they smell like?
What sound did you hear as they burst?
Did the bubbles feel different on your face, hands and arms?
How did it make you feel when you saw your 'worry bubble' burst?

Activity 1.2

Teddy-on-Your-Tummy Breathing

Breathing from your diaphragm allows you to take in more air and breathe more deeply and slowly, calming down the nervous system. When we breathe in this way our shoulders should stay down, and our abdomen should expand. 'Teddy-bear breathing' can be a lovely way to teach children this skill.

Ask your child to lie on the floor in a comfortable position on their back. Place their favourite teddy on their tummy and ask them to breathe in through their nose so that their tummy expands and the bear lifts up towards the ceiling. See if they can hold the bear up for a few seconds and then breathe out slowly through their mouths to bring the bear back down.

Reflection

How did that feel?

If it felt relaxing and fun, try breathing this way next time you are feeling worried to help you to feel calm!

Activity 1.3

Emotions Scale

Sometimes it can feel like children go from feeling calm, to a full-throttle meltdown in a matter of seconds. Helping children to understand and communicate the feelings that they have in between, can help to reduce the frequency and intensity of those big emotions.

Using the scale below, ask your child where they are on the scale. Have it somewhere to hand so that the child can start to indicate which character they are whenever they feel stressed and use the 'Calm-Down' Cards (see Activity 5.6) to teach them how to bring themselves back to feeling settled.

<table>
<tr><td rowspan="4">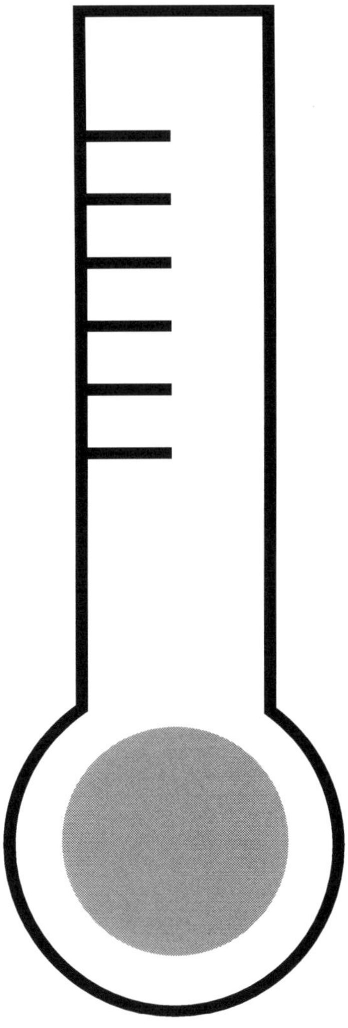</td><td></td><td>Panic
Out-of-control
Anger</td></tr>
<tr><td></td><td>Anxious
Wobbly
Fidgety</td></tr>
<tr><td></td><td>Happy
Calm
Settled</td></tr>
<tr><td></td><td>Sad
Tired
Bored</td></tr>
</table>

Which character are you on this scale?
If you are not feeling great, what could you do to help you cope better?

Activity 1.4

The Calm Box

When children are not feeling emotionally regulated, having some quiet time with some calming activities or objects can help. Activities that are distracting but low-challenge are ideal, and objects that calm the senses can be helpful.

Help your child to make their very own 'Calm Box' for when they are experiencing big emotions.

Making it with them will also help them to gain feelings of control and predictability, which can, in itself, be calming.

Make a box full of things that please you and help you feel calmer when you are low, or feeling out of control.

First decorate your box and then chose things to put inside it. You could choose . . .

- A mindful colouring sheet
- Felt-tip pens
- A snow-globe
- A cuddly toy
- Lavender-scented playdough

Activity 1.5

Emotions Board Game

Two to four people can play this game, using a dice and a different coloured counter for each person.

Rules

1. The youngest player starts by rolling the dice and moving forward the number of places shown on the dice.
2. When you reach a square, read the emotion, make the face for that emotion, and tell the other players about a time when you felt that emotion.
3. The next person rolls the dice, and so on. The winner is the first player to reach the end.

Activity 1.5

Emotions Board Game

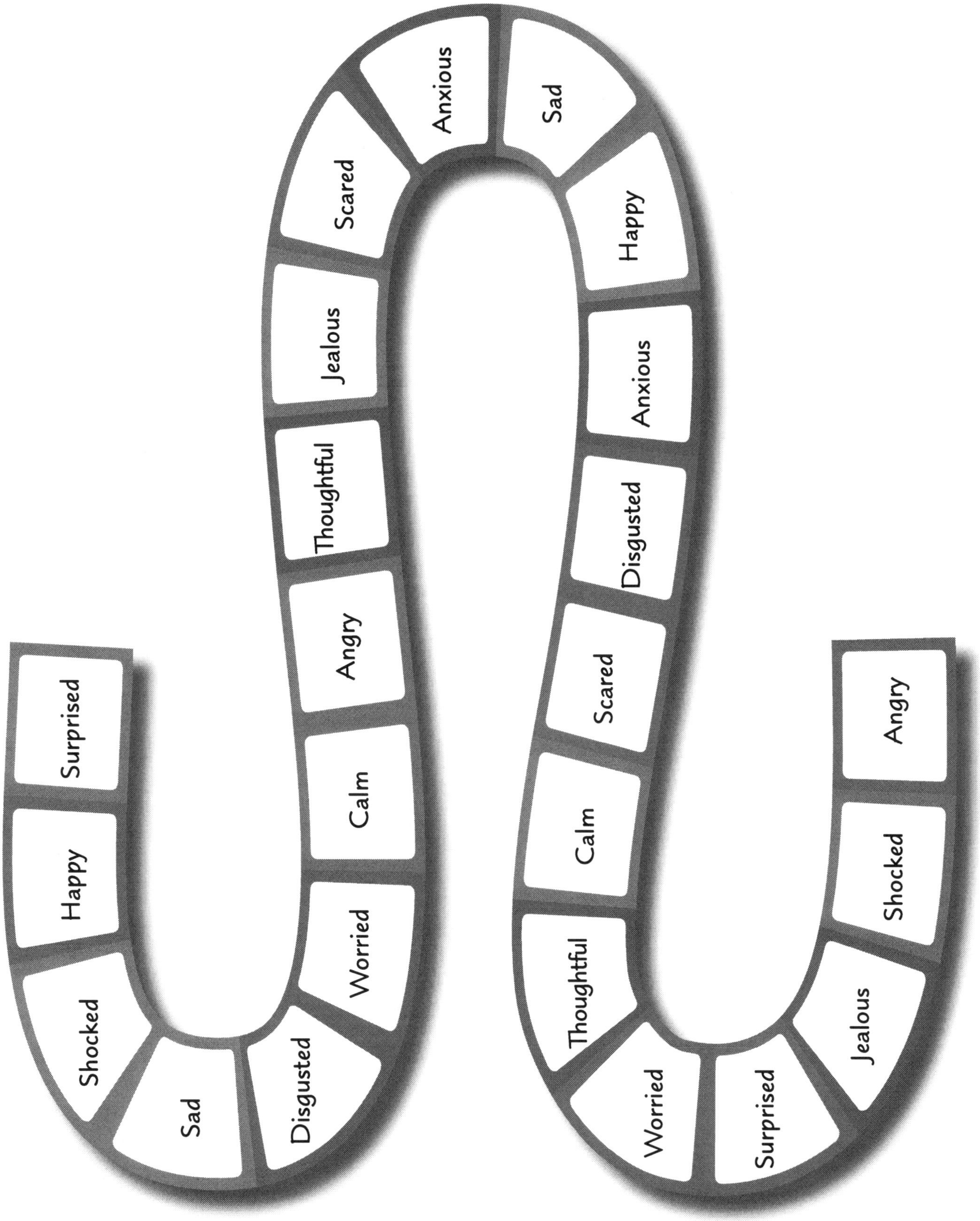

Page 2 of 2

Activity 1.6

Describing Emotions

You will need an assortment of stones or buttons for this activity, in different shapes, sizes, textures and colours.

Give the child the stones or buttons you have chosen and ask them to pick out one that would represent them when they feel angry, happy, sad and worried. For each, ask them why they chose the one that they did. This may help you to understand how they experience each emotion, and also develop the child's skills in being able to verbalise their big emotions.

Activity 1.7

Animal Yoga

Try going outside and doing these yoga poses. Remember as you hold each pose to focus on taking nice slow, deep breaths in through the nose (count to 4) and out through the mouth (count to 4).

Elephant Pose

Put your feet wide apart and clasp your hands together in front of you with straight arms, like an elephant's trunk. Bend forward from your hips to dip your trunk into the water. Then, as you breathe in, bring your body back up and stretch your arms up to the sky to spray out the water.

Lion Pose

Kneel and sit your bottom down on your heels. Place your hand on your knees and pretend they are claws. Breathe in through your nose, open your mouth and put out your tongue. As you breathe out, make the loudest roar that you can!

Dog Pose

Place your hands on the floor and walk your feet back so that you are in a triangle shape with your bottom in the air. Bend your knees, push your hips back away from your hands, and then ease your heels down towards the ground. Remember to give your tail a wag!

Snake Pose

Lie on your tummy and put your hands either side of your chest. Breathe in as you push your body up, keeping your hips on the ground. Then breathe out as you 'hisssssssss!'

Activity 1.8

Mindful Senses Scavenger Hunt

Taking time to notice what you sense around you in the present moment can help to ground you and reduce uncomfortable emotions, such as anxiety or frustration.

See if you can go out and find the following things.
Tick them off as you go . . .

Items	Tick
Hear a bird singing How many different birds can you hear? What do you think they are saying?	
A leaf What sound does it make when you hold it in your hand? How does it feel against your skin?	
A beautiful flower Look carefully and write down all of the colours that you can see.	
An insect How many legs does it have?	
Something that smells nice What does it smell like?	
Something shiny If you can touch it, does it feel hot or cold?	
A stick Does it float if you put it in water?	

Activity 1.9

Sensory Calming

Different activities work well for different children, depending upon their sensory profile. Experiment with these to see which help your child to feel calmer and encourage them to use these strategies when needed.

- Sit the child on a rocking chair, gym ball, or on your knee, and gently rock back and forth, slowly and rhythmically. Try resting the child's head comfortably to the side, and placing something weighted on their lap (e.g., a small bean bag).
- Try placing a star high up on the wall and asking the child to reach up and touch the star with both hands, pushing against the wall for 10 seconds.
- Music can be both calming and exciting. Listen to different music with the child to see how each type makes them feel. When you find one that is relaxing, encourage them to lie down, close their eyes and focus on the music.
- Certain smells can be relaxing (e.g., vanilla, lavender and rose). Try adding these to playdough, or to their bath to help them to relax.
- Taking deep breaths and blowing out through a straw can help to calm some children down. Try this in a cup of soapy water and watch the bubbles.

Activity 1.10

Mood Tracker Colouring

Encourage your child to notice and verbally label when they are feeling different emotions. When they feel them, they can colour in one of the scales on the handout fish with the corresponding colour. Children sometimes notice the big uncomfortable emotions more easily, so they may need you to help them to notice when they are feeling happy, calm and loved.

Tell them that they can use: blue for sadness; red for anger; yellow for happiness; green for worry; purple for calm; and pink for love

---

My Moody Fish

Whenever you feel an emotion, try to describe it with a colour and use that colour to fill in a scale on your moody fish. You can use:

blue for sadness
red for anger
yellow for happiness
green for worry
purple for calm
pink for love

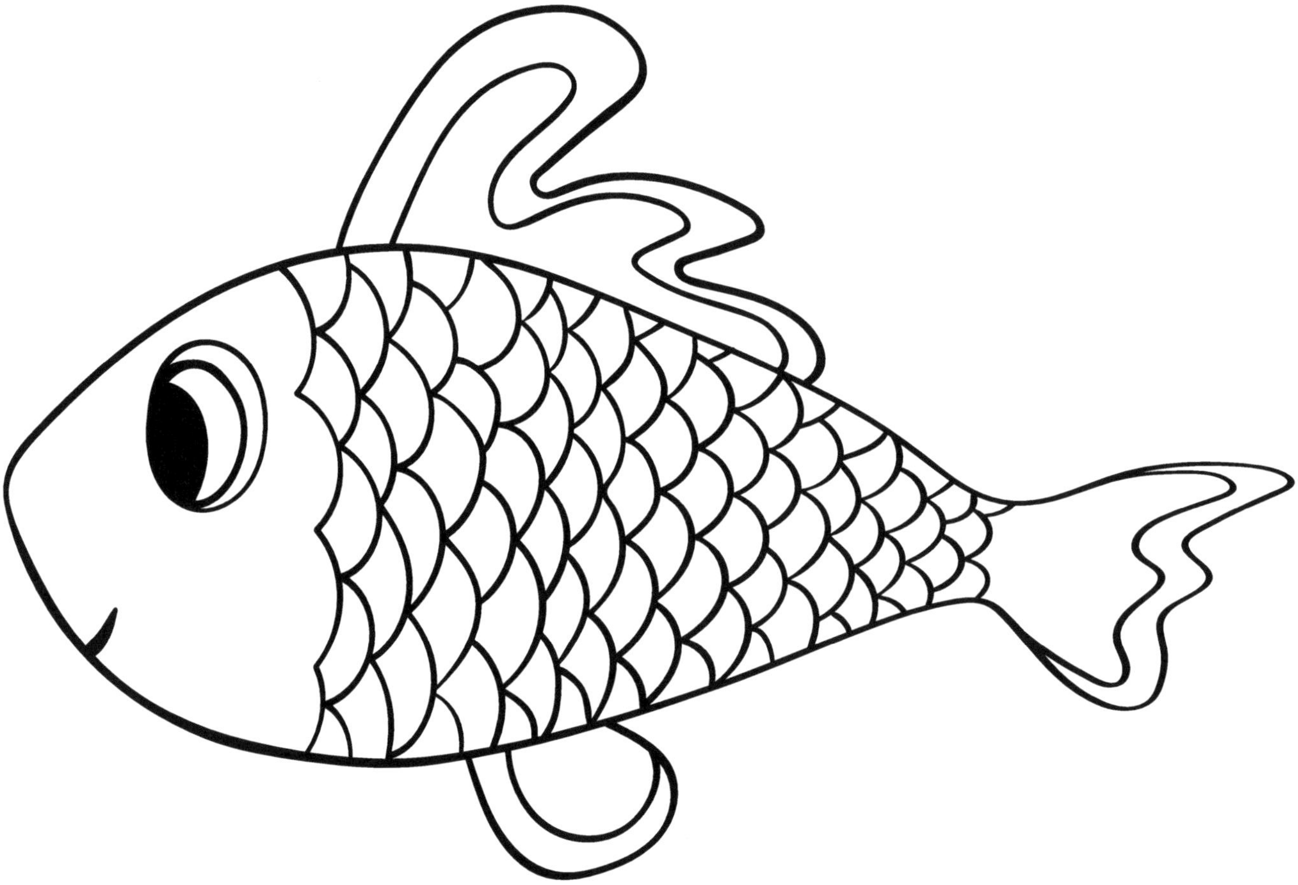

2 Resilience-Building Activities

Resilience is defined as 'the process of adapting well in the face of adversity' (American Psychological Association, 2012), and is sometimes referred to as our ability to 'bounce back' from adversity. It is important to note there are not 'resilient children' and 'less resilient children'; resilience refers to the interaction between the particular situation and the person experiencing that situation. Another essential factor is the adversity, as we cannot respond in a resilient way if we are protected from all challenges and negative experiences. Children are often quoted as being naturally resilient, but research into adverse childhood experiences and the impact that they have, suggests otherwise. Rather, it may be that children are just less able to process and demonstrate the negative emotions that they feel until later in life.

The likelihood of being able to respond with resilience can be thought of as being somewhat dependent upon the relative weight of risk factors and protective factors. Risk factors include family conflict, abuse or neglect, experiencing trauma, and living in poverty. Conversely, the Young Minds Interactive Resilience Framework provides a useful way for us to understand the factors that may help to protect the child from adversity and make it more likely that they will 'bounce back'. These include:

- Promoting a sense of belonging
- Maintaining a web of positive relationships
- Predicting good experiences and instilling a sense of hope
- Highlighting achievements
- Promoting bravery
- Helping children to problem-solve
- Thinking positively
- Being able to understand their own and others' feelings

All of these factors are things that can be promoted for any child and we hope that the activities within this chapter will help you to harness and develop these.

Activity 2.1

Draw a Coping Character

Think about a character who copes well with their worries. What would they look like? What would their name be? Draw them below . . .

What does this character do to overcome his worries?

____

____

In what ways are you similar to this character?

____

____

Activity 2.2

What Makes Me Happy?

This is my face when I'm feeling really happy . . .

Think about all the things that you do for fun? What makes you happy?

What three things made you feel most happy today?

1 ______________________________

2 ______________________________

3 ______________________________

Activity 2.3

It's Good to Talk

Make a list of all the people that you can talk to about your feelings . . .

____

____

____

____

____

What makes those people special?

	Name	**Tick**
They listen well		
They make me feel loved		
They are there when I need them		
They make me feel happy		
They make me feel calm		
Something else: ________________ ________________ ________________ ________________ ________________		

Activity 2.3

It's Good to Talk

What words might you use if you needed to talk to them about your feelings?

I'm feeling worried ☐

I need to talk to you about something important ☐

I need your help ☐

I feel sad ☐

Something else . . . ______________________________

____

____

______________________________ ☐

How do you feel when you've talked to someone about how you feel? Circle all the emotions you might feel.

Happy	Calm	Relieved
Sad	Worried	Loved

Activity 2.4

People Who Care

Knowing that we have people around us who we can rely on for support can help us to feel more secure in our ability to cope.

Draw or name all of the people around you that you can rely on.

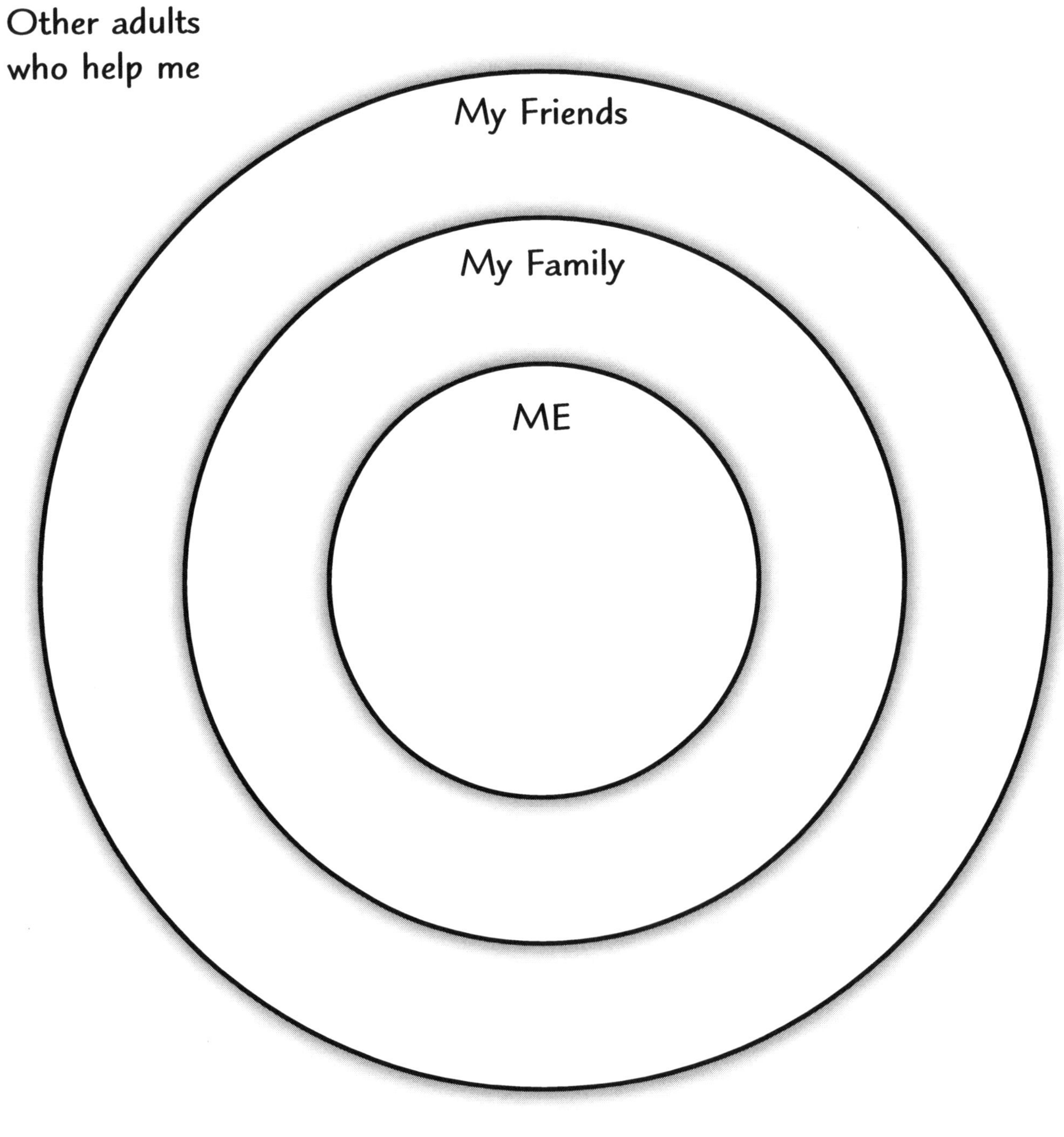

Activity 2.5

Miracle Question

Imagine that tonight while you are sleeping, a miracle happens that makes your life better.

Think for a moment and tell me what the miracle is . . .

How is life going to be different now? Draw what it will look like.

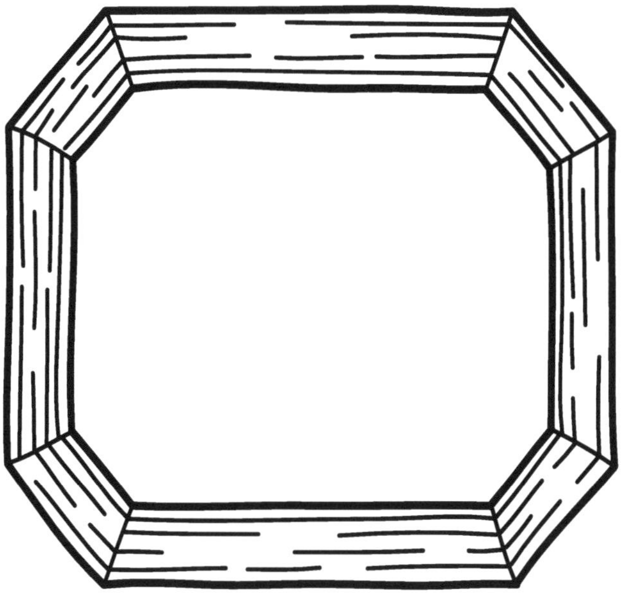

What's the first thing you'll notice when you wake up in the morning?

Activity 2.6

Hopes, Dreams & Wishes

What do you want to be when you grow up?

What do you wish for your family?

What is your biggest wish?

What do you wish for your friend?

Activity 2.7

My Gratitude Diary

Draw and label things you are grateful for. These could be your mum, or dad, or teacher. You could think about things you need every day, like food, friends and happy times.

Make a picture book and record 3 things you are grateful for each day.

Page 1 of 2

Activity 2.7

My Gratitude Diary

Page 2 of 2

Activity 2.8

My Happiness Shield

Draw the things that make you feel better when you have been sad or upset. Next time you feel sad use your shield and visualise it giving you protection

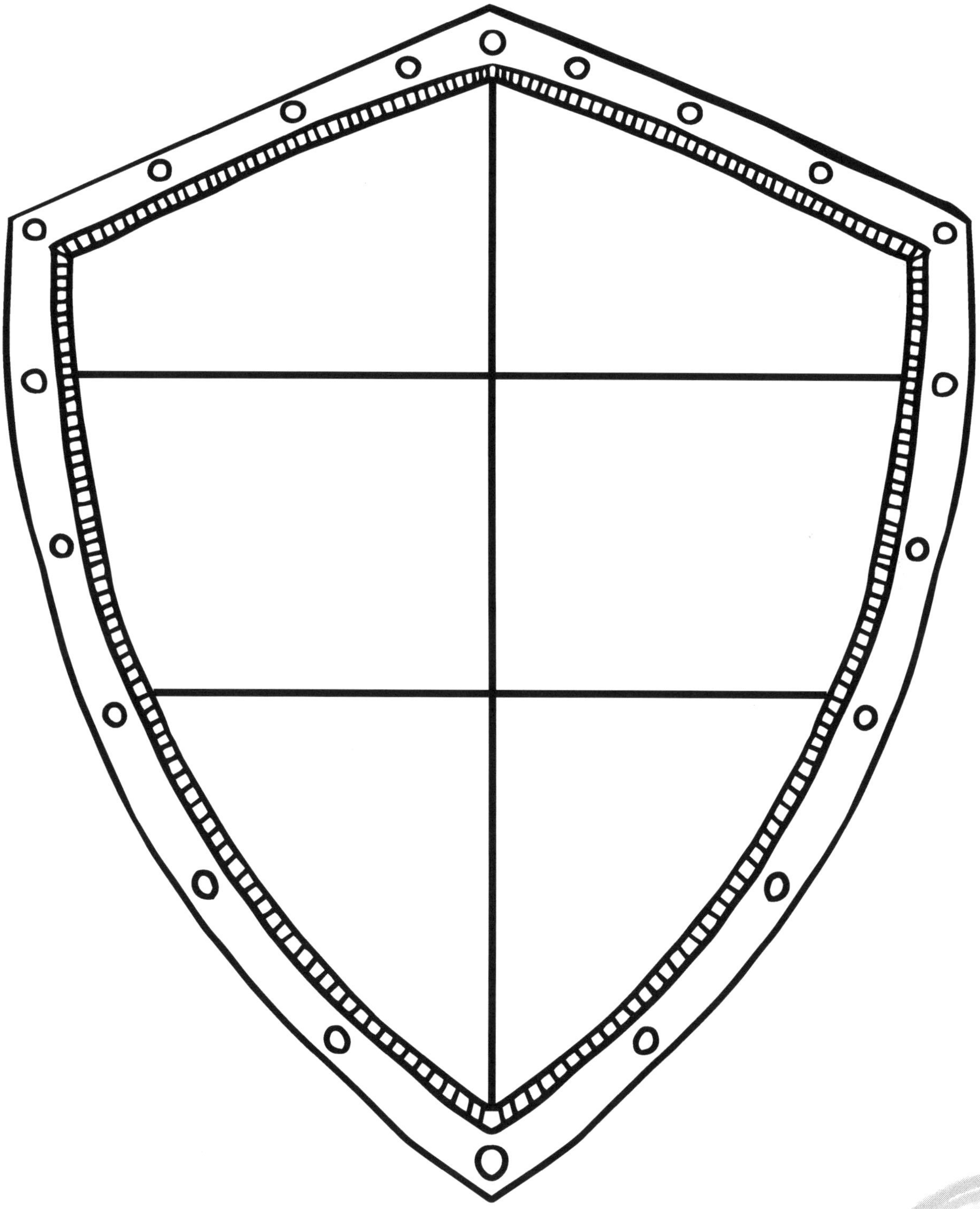

Activity 2.9

Happy Memories Collage

Remembering past events, situations or people with love and affection and in a positive way is a very important way of maintaining wellbeing. It is particularly useful to develop the ability to transport yourself to positive past times when things get tough or challenging.

Ask the child to recall as many happy times as they can and to make a collage of these events using photographs, scraps of material and pictures from magazines.

Next time they feel sad or lonely they can look at the pictures and relive the happy moments, which will remind them that times are not always bad.

Activity 2.10

My Golden Scroll

Sometimes we forget to think about the positive or good things that happen – NOT GOOD!

Every evening, think of one thing (at least) that has happened that made you feel good.

Record these on your golden scroll in words and pictures.

At the end of the week LOOK at the scroll and relive all these positive moments!

3 Self-Esteem & Social Skills Activities

Self-Esteem

Self-esteem is a term used to reflect a person's overall emotional evaluation of their own worth. According to educational psychologist, Michele Borba (2003), rather than being a unitary concept, self-esteem can be thought of as having five sequential components, or 'building blocks'. These are as follows:

- **Security.** This refers to feelings of safety and assuredness. The ability to trust and rely on others and to feel secure within appropriate boundaries.
- **Selfhood.** This refers to having a realistic and accurate image of who you are and what makes you an individual.
- **Affiliation.** This refers to having a sense of belonging and feeling respected, appreciated and accepted by others, particularly within the relationships that are most important to you.
- **Mission.** Refers to feeling motivated and having a sense of purpose.
- **Competence.** Refers to having a sense of achievement and success. It also involves being able to identify strengths and feel that these are valued and important, as well as accepting areas of relative weakness.

Using this description, it is clear to see that the pandemic may have impacted children's self-esteem. The message to 'stay home' and 'social distance' may have made children feel less safe, while many of their social and family relationships may have been temporarily lost; and with less immediate face-to-face feedback from school staff, many may have felt less competent and motivated.

Social Skills

The disease control measures implemented during the pandemic have meant that the interactions which children and adolescents have had with family and friends outside of the home have often been through virtual means. The CO-SPACE study (Dodd, Westbrook & Lawrence, 2020) explored the impact of lockdown on young children (aged 2 to 4) and families, and found that 91 per cent of children had communicated with family outside of the home via video call. However, only 49 per cent had communicated in this way with friends, and not seeing their friends was the most commonly reported worry of the pre-school children themselves. With 47 per cent of the sample having other children in the home to play with, it is unsurprising that the emotional wellbeing of their children was amongst the top concerns of the parents.

These resources have been designed to support children in re-building their self-esteem and developing their social skills in preparation for the return to school and beyond

Activity 3.1

What Makes a Good Friend?

Have a thought-storm session with the child and try to identify all the qualities you can think of together that would make a good friend.

Give the child some prompts:

- A friend is someone who plays nicely
- A friend takes turns
- A friend is kind
- A friend takes care of you if you hurt yourself
- A friend makes you smile
- A friend makes you feel happy

You can record these on a special friendship poster.

As a follow up you could identify all the things that do *not* make a good friend.

Activity 3.2

Playing

Look at all of these children playing . . .

Which child is most like you? Why?

____

____

Which child would you most like to be? Why?

____

____

Are there any children that you think you would like to be friends with? Why?

____

____

Activity 3.3

Kindness

Good friends are kind.

Think of all the times when you have been kind to others. What did they do? How did they feel? What did they say?

Then plan a kind thing that you can do for someone else today.

Record this in a 'Kind Acts Journal'. You can use the outline below if you like.

Today I will be kind.

I will ____

Activity 3.4

My Mirror

Look into a mirror and draw what you can see.

Then think about what you have achieved – the things that you can do that you are proud of! What skills do you have? Can you ride a bike? Colour in a picture? Sing? Run fast?

Stop and think! Make a list of all your achievements and skills, or draw pictures of you doing those things.

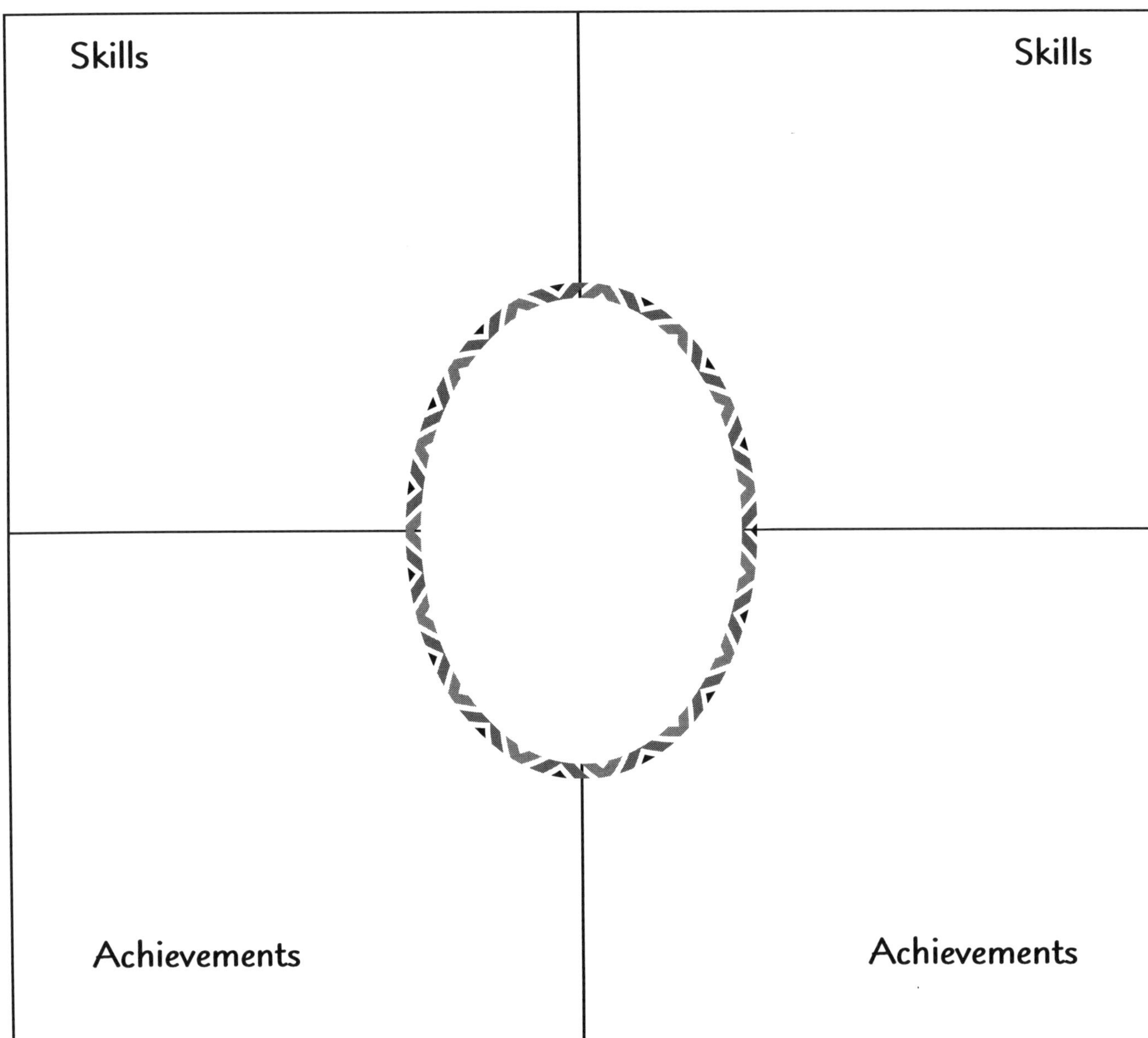

Activity 3.5

Things I Like About Me!

Draw and label the things you like about yourself and things that make you feel happy, positive and healthy.

Share your ideas with a partner. How are you the same? How are you different?

Activity 3.6

Things I Can Do for Others

Draw a picture of yourself to stick in the middle of the page.

Then write or draw all the things you can do for others around your portrait . . .

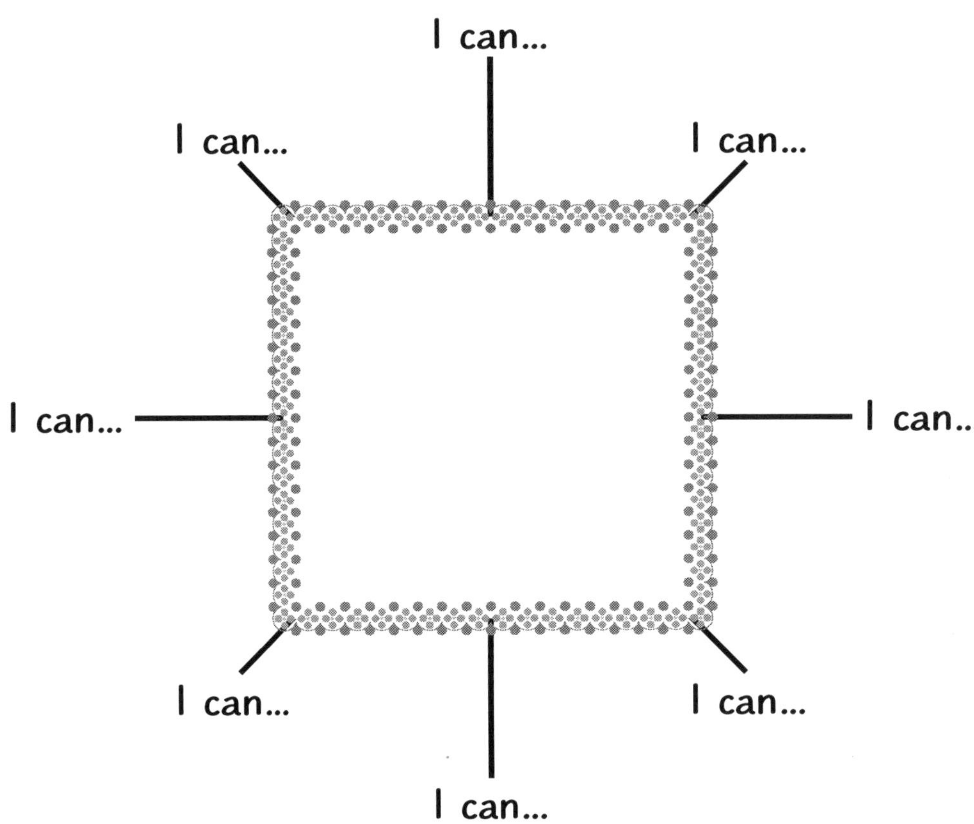

Activity 3.7

Friendship Bracelets & Badges

Ask the child to design and make a friendship bracelet or badge to give to a special friend.

They can draw this out first and then make use of beads, card, sequins, sewing threads, and so on, to actually make the object.

Ask the child to think about why they have chosen the person they want to give their token of friendship to – and what they would like to say to them when they give them their gift.

Activity 3.8

My Secret Mirror!

Draw yourself in the mirror. Then draw the things that other people may not know about you around the outside of the mirror – this is your secret self!

Activity 3.9

Personal Compliments: I Am a Star!

Pay yourself 5 compliments – YOU CAN!

Just think about all the things you like about yourself – plan and talk!!

Then draw and write in the stars.

I am
a star
because ...

I am
a star
because ...

Page 1 of 2

Activity 3.9

Personal Compliments: I Am a Star!

I am
a star
because ...

I am
a star
because ...

I am
a star
because ...

Activity 3.10

Friendship Rules

Think about why we need to have rules to keep us all safe and happy. Then work with the child to identify some key Friendship Rules.

These can be framed as a list of 'dos'. For example:

- Do take turns
- Do say kind things
- Do share
- Do think about how others feel
- Do take care of others who are hurt

Make a lovely poster of these rules and illustrate the poster with pictures of good friends.

4 Effective Thinking Activities

Cognitive Behavioural Therapy

Helping children become aware of the ways in which thoughts can influence emotions and behaviour is one of the most valuable lessons we can give them. Cognitive Behavioural therapy (CBT) can help children to reframe how they identify, interpret and evaluate their emotional and behavioural reactions to negative experiences (Rae, 2016).

Realising that emotions and behaviours can be regulated and managed is empowering and can lead to improvements in self-control, emotion regulation, coping skills, and emotional awareness during this critical developmental stage.

Cognitive Behavioural Therapy (CBT) has been found to be effective for a range of mental health problems, including mood-related disorders (e.g., depression, low self-esteem, low confidence) and anxiety-related problems (e.g., anxiety, panic, eating disorders – such as anorexia nervosa, bulimia nervosa, binge-eating – obsessive compulsive disorder (OCD), post-traumatic stress disorder (PTSD)) and other emotional and behavioural problems (e.g., bereavement, relationship problems, sleep disorders).

The focus

CBT focuses on the role that thoughts play regarding both emotions and behaviour and advocates that changes in thought processes can have a significant effect upon altering behaviours. CBT is based on the idea that the way we think about situations can affect the way we feel and behave. For example, if you interpret a situation negatively then you might experience negative emotions as a result, and those bad feelings might then lead you to behave in a certain way.

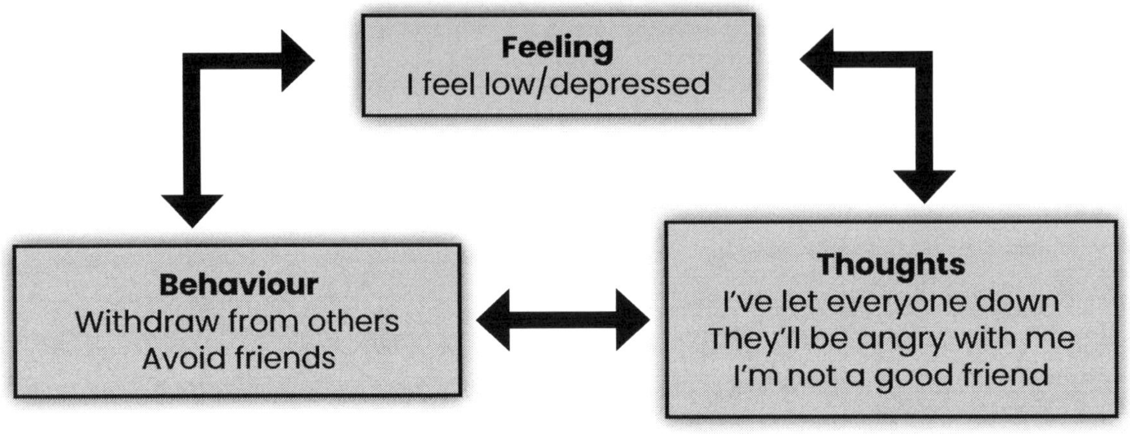

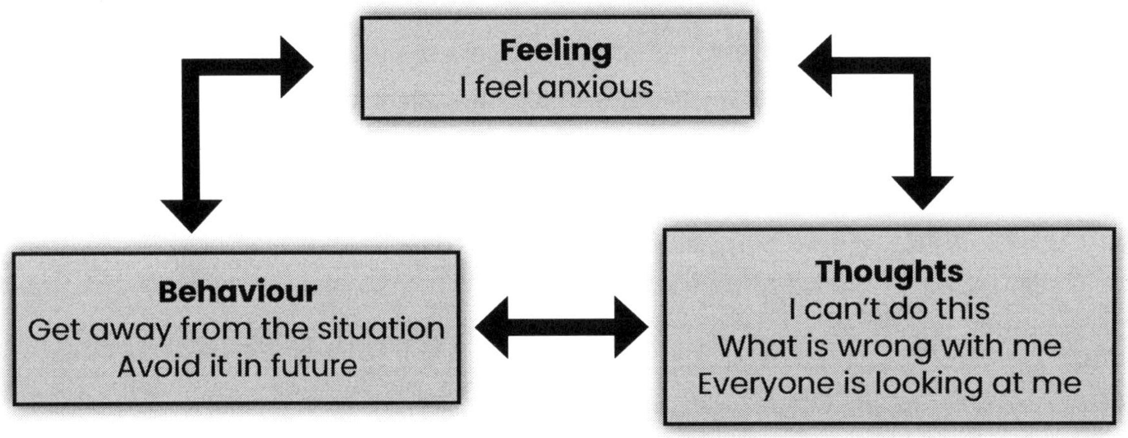

This approach provides individuals with a way of talking about themselves, their world and the people who inhabit it, so that they are more able to understand how their behaviour affects both their thoughts and feelings.

The tools and strategies employed in this approach are easily accessible to children and young people alike.

The issue

We know that young people are frequently flooded with anxious and negative thoughts and doubts. These messages will often reinforce a state of inadequacy and/or low levels of self-esteem. The process of CBT helps to support young people in reconsidering these negative assumptions. It also allows them to *learn how* to change their self-perceptions in order to improve their mental and emotional state – this is the key aim of this kind of intervention. Changing negative thought patterns or opinions will ultimately help young people to become more able to control and change their behaviours, but this does take practice.

ABC

The CBT approach breaks a problem into three smaller parts:

A is the **activating event**, often referred to as the 'trigger' – the thing that causes you to engage in the negative thinking.

B represents these negative **beliefs**, which can include thoughts, rules and demands, and the meanings the individual attaches to both external and internal events.

C is for the **consequences**, or emotions, and the behaviours and physical sensations accompanying these different emotions. It is important to highlight and discuss with children how the way that they think about a problem can affect how they feel physically and emotionally. It can also alter what they do about it. Therefore, the key aim for CBT is to break the negative, vicious cycle that some students may find themselves in. For example, if you think that you will get your work wrong you feel angry, and then you do not give it a try in case it is wrong.

Cognitive Restructuring

The purpose of this technique is to change cognitive distortions (irrational negative thoughts and beliefs someone has about different situations) and to increase positive self-talk. Normally, there will be some type of event that will trigger the irrational thought. While the event cannot be changed, the way the child looks at the event can be. An example could be a child working hard on a project or test and not receiving as high a grade as they expected. A child will see their efforts as useless and may start to think, 'I'm useless', or 'There is no point in trying.' Other irrational negative thoughts could include:

- I can't do anything well
- Things never work out for me
- Nobody likes me
- I'm dumb
- Something's wrong with me
- I can't make any friends
- I'm worthless

These thoughts need to be recognised and countered. Often the child will not even realise exactly what they are saying and how irrational these thoughts are. It is one of the main focuses of this technique to recognise the thoughts that will cause the anxiety. However, it is also important to not counter them with equally irrational positive thoughts. For example, it would not be proper to counter, 'Nobody likes me', with, 'No, everyone *does* like you.' It is important to be **realistic** with the replacement thought. 'Well not *everyone* likes you, but you know some people do; your mother and sister love you', would be a better approach.

It is important that these negative attitudes do not form part of the child's habitual thought patterns. The child will begin to believe them fully and this leads to depression, feelings of worthlessness, and a loss of direction. It could also precipitate avoidance or even panic attacks in the child. You can correct the child whenever you hear it as a part of their speech, and work to have them recognise it themselves. Encourage them to recognise the good things they do instead. Make sure they know there is no shame in congratulating themselves for a job well done.

Activity 4.1

What Can I Control?

Sometimes we worry about things we cannot control. This does not help us or reduce our anxiety. Going to a new school or classroom, or doing something new for the first time can be a challenge.

We need to help children to focus instead on things they *can* control.

Help the child to make a list of the things that are within their control, acting as their scribe. Then ask them to illustrate their list to make it a visual reminder of the important areas where they do have some control.

They might include the following:

- Being kind
- Good sitting
- Good listening
- Sharing
- Working hard
- Trying hard
- Telling an adult if I am worried
- Showing how I feel
- Using my 'calm box' if I get stressed

Activity 4.2

Negative Thoughts

Sometimes we have sad thoughts or think things are true when they are not.

Have a look at the thoughts in the bubbles and discuss them. Have you thought like this and were you right?

I thought it was my fault

I thought my friend didn't like me

I thought my teacher was angry with me

I thought I was horrid

I thought I couldn't do the work

I thought people were unkind to me

I thought no one wanted to play with me

Remember that sometimes we think something – but we may not be right!

Our negative thoughts are not always true!

Activity 4.3

Happy & Positive Thoughts

If we have positive thoughts about ourselves and others we will tend to feel happier.

Work with your child to record 10 happy and positive thoughts they have about themselves and others, using the spaces below.

Thought 1 is ______________________________

Thought 2 is ______________________________

Thought 3 is ______________________________

Thought 4 is ______________________________

Thought 5 is ______________________________

Thought 6 is ______________________________

Thought 7 is ______________________________

Thought 8 is ______________________________

Thought 9 is ______________________________

Thought 10 is ______________________________

Activity 4.4

Thoughts, Feelings & Behaviours

Help the child to see the links between how they think, feel and behave.

Use the example in the illustration below.

Thought – Ben thought he was bad at colouring

Feeling – Ben felt silly and sad when his teacher asked him to colour the picture

Behaviour – Ben screwed up his paper and did not colour the picture

Ask the child to make their own version and identify a time when they felt sad that they could not do something.

Then try to think about what they could have done differently. Who might have helped them?

Activity 4.5

Pea Scale

Sometimes problems and worries can feel very small, like a pea, and at other times they feel very big, like a pumpkin.

Think about a problem that you have . . .

Where would it be on the scale of vegetables?

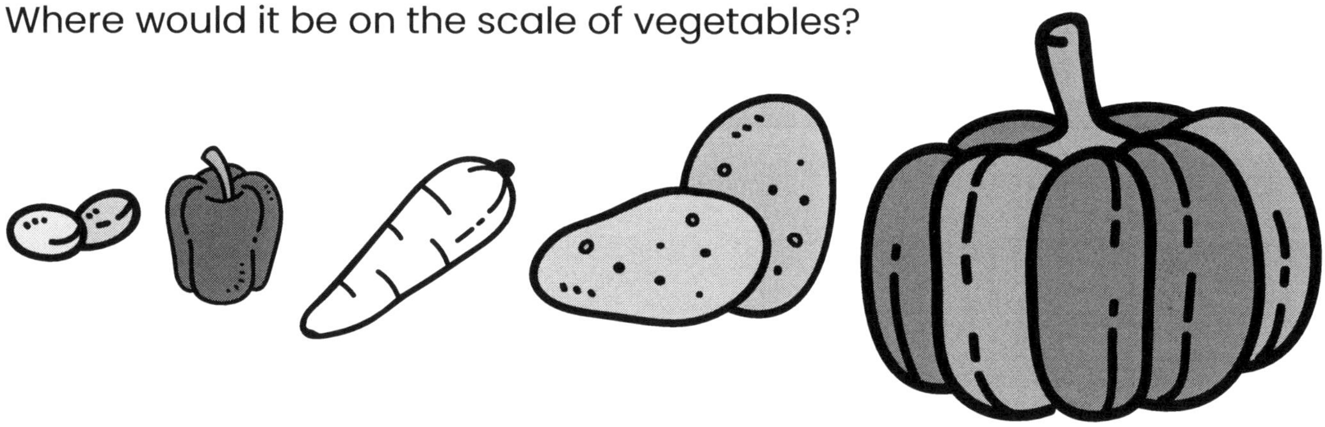

Pea Pepper Parsnip Potato Pumpkin

What would need to happen to make your worry seem smaller?

What size might your parent or carer think your worry is?

What size might your teacher think your worry is?

Activity 4.6

My Positive Picture Book

Make a positive picture book with the child. Cut out 'happy times' pictures from a range of magazines, comics, and so on, and stick one into the book for each day of the week.

Then write the story together for the week.

For example:

On Monday they were happy because . . .
On Tuesday they were happy because . . .

Then ask the child to think of one happy thought they had for each day of the week and record this underneath each of the pictures.

Activity 4.7

Find the Facts

You **may** think your work is not good.
But this may not be true.
You **may** be wrong.

Find the facts. Be a 'thought detective'!
What negative thought do you have about yourself?

What I think:

____

Now **ASK** five people to say what **they** think.

Record what they think on the chart. Put the name of each person you've asked first, and then record their answer.

What other people think . . .

1 ____

____

2 ____

____

3 ____

____

4 ____

____

5 ____

____

Take some time to discuss this. How much do you believe your thought now?

Activity 4.8

Positive Post-Its

On each post-it note draw and label a happy and positive thought.

See how many you can complete in one day.

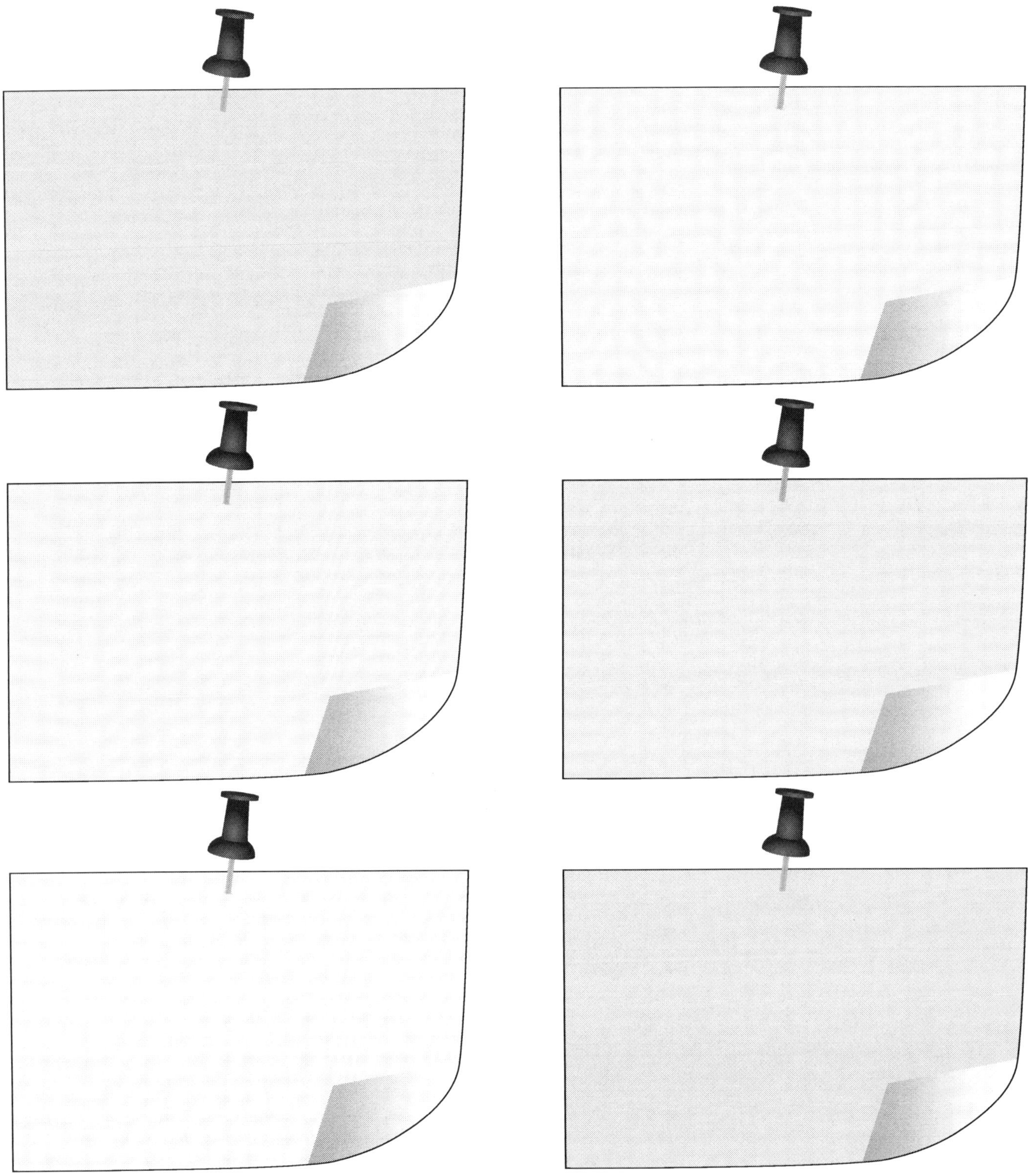

Activity 4.9

Mirror Talk

Take a mirror and look carefully at yourself, and then say all the good things you can see.

Practise this together with the child and give them some prompts if they find it difficult, for example:

- I can see a happy face
- I can see kind eyes
- I can see a lovely smile
- I can see someone I want to be friends with
- I can see someone who tries hard
- I can see someone who is a good friend

Activity 4.10

Affirmation Cards

Make a range of Affirmation Cards. The child could draw lovely illustrations, or you could collect these from magazines to put on the front of each card (e.g., lovely scenery, happy people, seascapes, etc.)

On the back of each card write an affirmation. These might include the following:

I am good	I am a good friend
I am kind	I am helpful
I am loved	I am strong
I am liked	I am brave

The child can look through these at the beginning of each day and pick one to keep in their pocket during the day. They can take it out and look at during the day, reminding themselves of their worth and how to feel good about themselves.

5 Anxiety-Busting Activities

What is Anxiety?

Anxiety is a normal response to a perceived threat and includes physical, emotional and mental responses, such as an increase in adrenalin, feelings of worry and confusion, and thoughts about danger and catastrophic outcomes. Normal levels of anxiety can assist people to be more focused and motivated, and to solve problems more efficiently. However, **chronic or high levels of anxiety** can reduce a person's capacity to respond appropriately or effectively to stressful situations or even normal routine activities. For example, a highly anxious person may experience constant physical feelings of panic and may seek to avoid anything that might trigger their anxiety (such as being alone, going to school, or talking in front of a group).

Anxiety may be triggered in many different ways. Sources of anxiety may include (but are not limited to) fear of:

- Social situations
- Negative evaluation and rejection
- Performing in public
- A specific object or situation (e.g., storms or lightning/thunder, insects, blood)
- Separation from a parent/carer
- A parent/carer being harmed
- Harm to oneself
- Academic performance and exams
- Starting school or work
- The future (what will happen, how it might turn out)

Anxiety may manifest as a number of physical symptoms, including muscle tension, shaking/trembling and heart palpitations, sweating/flushing, or feeling very hot or cold, amongst many others. In addition, children and young people experiencing anxiety may display a number of behavioural symptoms, including withdrawing from friends and family, avoidance of particular situations and negative thoughts or pessimism. Due to the way in which the brain develops, young children are particularly prone to responding with heightened emotions and find it more difficult to understand or regulate these emotions.

Signs of anxiety in young children may include:

- Increased tantrums/ meltdowns
- Regression (e.g., in toileting)
- Changes in eating
- Difficulty sleeping
- Being clingy
- More tearful
- Complaining of tummy aches, or feeling unwell

Top Tips for Supporting Young Children who Are Feeling Anxious

1 Often young children lack the emotional vocabulary to be able to communicate their feelings to you, and therefore they show their anxiety through their behaviour (e.g., tantrums or meltdowns, controlling behaviour, defiance). Labelling their emotions for them and empathising can really help them to start to build up this vocabulary so that they can communicate in a more adaptive way as they develop. (See Appendix 4, 'Emotion Coaching Information Sheet'.)

2 Toddlers and young children have very little control and autonomy over anything and this can mean that they become overwhelmed, anxious and easily frustrated. Where possible, provide routine and consistency and allow them to feel a sense of control through being given choices.

3 Ensure that you have a good bedtime routine in place, which helps them to calm down. For example, a bath around an hour before bed to ensure optimal core body temperature for a restful night's sleep, no screens before bed, and read them a bedtime story to help them to settle. Sleep allows us to better regulate our emotions, so a well-rested toddler is more likely to be a calm one!

4 Help them to face things that make them anxious by gently teaching them to problem-solve around their fears. For example, if they are afraid of dogs, model calm behaviour around a known, calm dog to show them that dogs are not always dangerous. This is much more empowering than protecting them and assisting them in avoiding the things that they are afraid of, as this sends the message that the feared situation is dangerous for them and that they cannot cope with it, meaning that the anxiety is more likely to persist.

5 Keep your calm! It can be exceptionally difficult to keep calm yourself when faced with an anxious child having a meltdown in the middle of the supermarket. Just try to remember that they get tired and overwhelmed easily, and they are still learning how to control those big emotions. It is our job to show them how.

Whilst anxiety is a normal reaction to stressful events or change, if you are concerned that anxiety is affecting your child's behaviour and thoughts every day and interfering with their ability to function socially, or at home or school, you should consult with a medical professional as this may be indicative of an anxiety disorder (see Appendix 3, 'Stress, Anxiety Disorder & Depression Information Sheet')

Activity 5.1

Worry Words

Young children often lack the emotional vocabulary to describe their uncomfortable feelings and tend to show these through their behaviour (e.g., crying, meltdowns, tantrums).

By helping your child to label these verbally, it can help them to reduce the intensity of their feelings and start to communicate their worries in a more adaptive way.

All of the words below are 'worry words' that might help describe how Billy Bear is feeling:

Anxious

Fearful

Scared

Worried

Panicky

Wobbly

Shaky

Nervous

Apprehensive

Can you think of any more words to describe how Billy Bear might be feeling?

____

Which word might you choose to describe how you feel at the following times? (It might be a word from above or a different 'feeling' word that you know.)

____

Page 1 of 2

Activity 5.1

Worry Words

1 When I have to go somewhere without my parent/carer, I feel

____

____

2 When I go somewhere new for the first time, I feel

____

____

3 When I have to say something in front of lots of people, I feel

____

____

When you feel wobbly in your tummy, have shaky legs like Billy Bear, and your heart is beating faster, which word will you choose to tell the adults how you are feeling?

Page 2 of 2

Activity 5.2

Which Animal Would Your Worry Be?

It can be helpful to externalise and depersonalise the worry, so that the child can separate themselves from the feeling and talk about it more objectively. Describing it as an animal may help them to talk to you about the feeling more easily.

If your worried feeling was an animal, which animal would it be?

How is that animal like you when you feel worried?

Activity 5.3

Making & Using Puppets

Puppets can be a great way of helping the child to role-play and explore different scenarios and feelings.

Cut out and stick the characters below on to lolly-sticks and have fun acting out the following scenarios with your child. Make sure you swap characters around so that your child gets an opportunity to verbalise the worries, but also a chance to be empowered through playing the helpful, calm, coping character.

Scenarios

1. Billy Bear is feeling worried about his first day at school. How can Daisy Dolphin help him to stay calm?
2. Billy Bear is feeling worried about the virus. How can Daisy Dolphin help him to feel better about it?
3. Now try a scenario that is specific to the worries that your child has. How might Daisy Dolphin be able to help if . . .

Activity 5.4

Why Are They Worried?

Sometimes children find it difficult to talk about things that are worrying them. By asking them to talk about someone else's worries, often they will give you some insight into their own worries, since children of this age find it difficult to imagine things from another perspective.

Look at the pictures below. How do you think they are feeling?

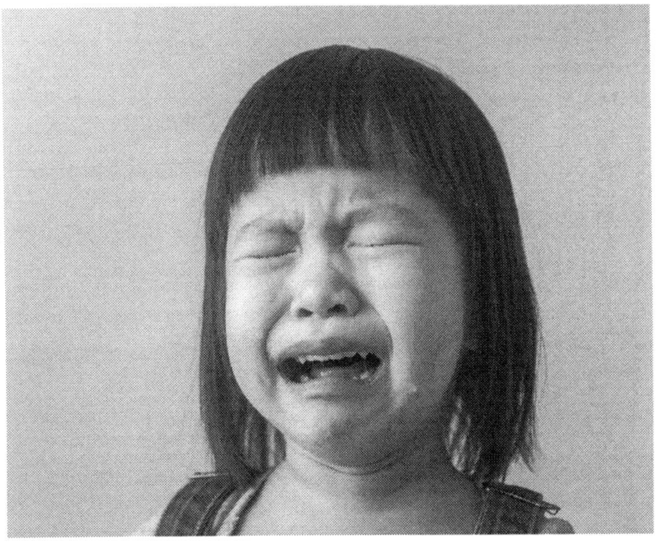

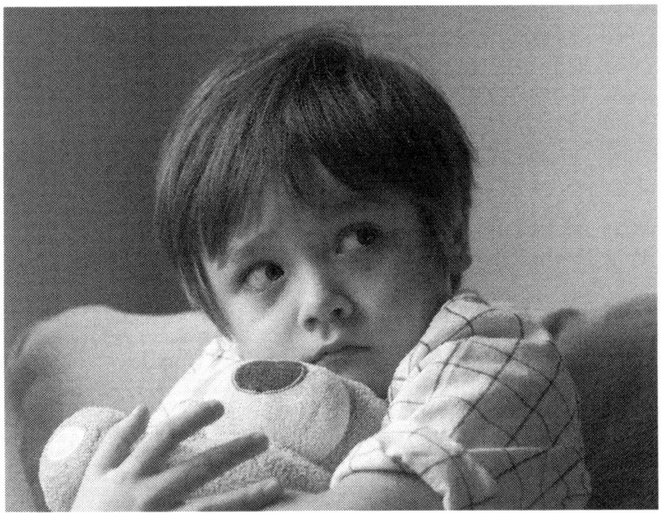

Why do you think they are feeling that way?

Activity 5.5

Body Language & Emotions

Put a circle around the characters that you think are feeling worried . . .

How do you know? What is it about their body or face that tells you that they are worried?

Activity 5.6

Calm-Down Cards

Use these 'Calm-Down' cards to remind children of strategies that they can use to help bring themselves back to a happy, settled, content state. These are particularly effective when used in conjunction with the Emotions Scale (Activity 1.3).

Discuss with your child those that would be useful to use when they are at the top, middle, or bottom of the Emotions Scale.

Take 10 deep breaths	Use my calm box	Go for a walk
Talk to someone	Ask for a hug	Listen to some music
Count slowly to 10	Do some star jumps	Have some quiet time

Activity 5.7

Worry Time

Sometimes for children who worry a lot, it can be helpful to schedule in some 'worry time' to think and talk through the things that are concerning them. This should be for a limited time and followed with a calming or fun activity.

It might help to write your worries in the bubbles below.

Use the following questions to help the child to talk about their worries:

- How worried do you feel about it? (Use the Pea Scale, Activity 4.5.)
- What would help you to feel less worried about it?
- How might you help Billy Bear if he felt worried about your worry?

Activity 5.8

Draw Your Safe Space

Imagine a place where you feel safe, happy and content.

Where would you be? What would it look like? What would you be doing? Who would be with you?

Draw your safe space below . . .

How could you make your bedroom or classroom more similar to this place? How might that make you feel?

Activity 5.9

How to Tell an Adult I'm Feeling Worried

It can feel difficult to find the words to tell someone that you are feeling worried. There are lots of ways to tell someone so that they can help. Which of these do you think you could try?

Say 'I'm feeling worried' It's good to use your words if you can, so that an adult knows how you feel and can help you if you need it.	**Show them a card** Some children find it helpful to have a green card for when they feel good and a red card for when they need help.
Have a special hand sign You could agree a special hand signal with your teacher, so that you can tell them easily when you are feeling worried.	**Have a secret pencil signal** If you want to send a message to your teacher in secret, you could use a green pencil on your desk when you feel okay and a red one when you are feeling worried.
Use the Emotions Scale You could have an Emotions Scale on your desk, so that you could show it to your teacher if you are starting to feel worried.	**Tell a friend** Sometimes it can feel hard to tell an adult how you are feeling, but you might be able to tell a friend.

Activity 5.10

What Does Worry Feel Like?

Young children often find it hard to express their worry because of all of the feelings that arise in the body that make them feel as if there is something physically wrong (e.g., shaking, feeling sick, headache, tummy ache).

Think about a time that felt scary. Think about the feelings in your head, chest, hands, legs and tummy. Draw on the bear to show how your body felt.

How do I know when I'm feeling worried?

____

____

6 Transition Activities

Whether you are supporting a child who is transitioning back to school, pre-school, or starting in Reception; think of transition as a process rather than a one-off event. They will need careful preparation beforehand and it may take a while before they feel settled. Change is a stressor for all of us and, when we already feel anxious, change can feel particularly overwhelming. According to neuroscientist, Dr Bruce Perry (2020), we are most able to tolerate change when it feels predictable and within our control. For this reason we have included some activities that will help you and your child to plan for changes, and maintain a consistent, predictable routine within your day.

We must not forget that this transition is likely to be harder than most, following all of the messages that children have received around 'staying safe at home', and the implicit suggestion that other children and adults pose a threat to us. Therefore, it is essential that children are supported in feeling that school, pre-school and the outside world are safe places to be, so that they have the confidence to explore, play and learn.

Separation anxiety is also very common in young children, and within the current pandemic, it is likely that some children will find it difficult to separate from their parents after so long together. It is important to accept, validate and empathise with the child, rather than trying to distract them away from their very understandable emotion.

The following general guidance may also be helpful in easing the transition:

- The child may benefit through having access to pictures of the school, their teachers, and opportunities to meet with other children in their class (even if done virtually). You could also prepare them by allowing them to try on their uniform and get used to their school shoes, as well as doing some test-runs of the journey to school.

- Communication between home and school/pre-school is key to ensure a smooth transition. Parents know their children the best and any transition document or meeting should allow for discussion of how the child shows their anxiety and what helps them to feel calm. At this time, it will also be essential to discuss their individual experience of lockdown and how this may impact upon the transition.

- Explore the theme of transition, change and resilience through play with the child, to help to provide a positive narrative around uncertainty and new beginnings.

Activity 6.1

Starting School

Make a list of all the things the child is looking forward to about going to school.

Reinforce how exciting it all is.

Then make a list of worries and record next to each one what the child can do if they experience these worries – who can help them, what they can do to help themselves.

Reinforce the fact that we need to talk so we can sort out worries and they do not stop us from having a lovely time at school.

- Things I am looking forward to in my exciting new school . . .
- My worries and things I can do about them . . .

Activity 6.2

The Hug Button

It is very common for children to struggle with separating from a parent or carer, as often they represent the child's safe base. This can be particularly difficult when the situation feels new, unfamiliar, or a change from the usual routine.

Try this technique to help your child to stay feeling connected to you and to allow them to explore the world with confidence when you are apart.

1 Draw a heart on the palm of your hand and one on the palm of your child's hand. This is a 'hug button'.

2 'Charge' the hug button by holding hands on the way to school.

3 Let your child know that anytime they are missing you, they can press the button to give you a hug.

4 After school, let them know about all the hugs that you sent and that you loved the hugs that they sent to you.

Top Tip: Draw a spare button somewhere on your child where it will not get rubbed or washed off!

Activity 6.3

Heart Strings

Even when we are apart, we are all connected to those that we love by Heart Strings. We can tug on these to let others know when we are missing them.

You might like to read the story 'The Invisible String' by Patrice Karst to your child to explore this idea further.

Draw yourself in the box below and then draw all of the people that you are connected to by strings of love. Love has no limits – you can add as many strings as you like!

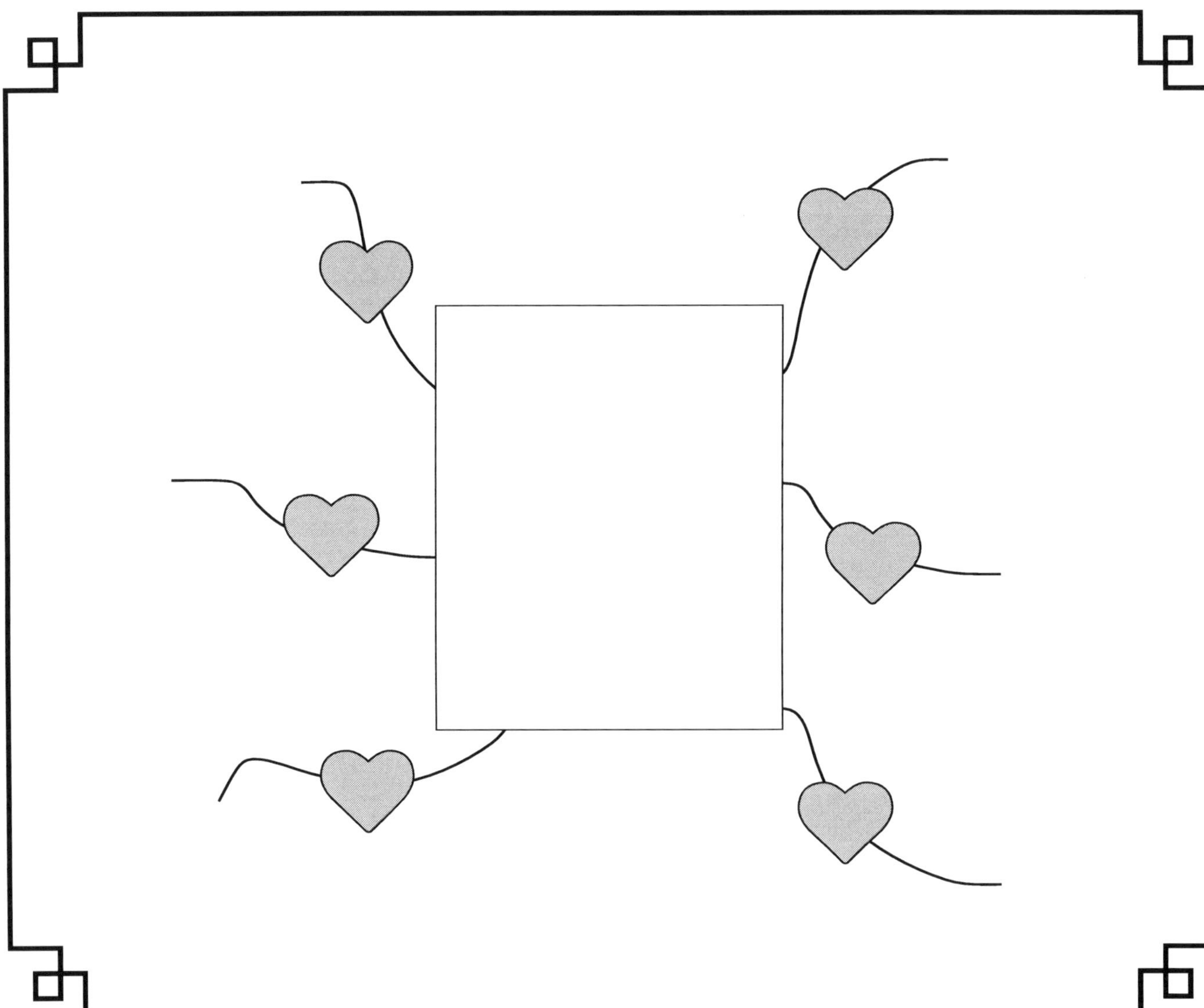

Activity 6.4

A Perfect Day at School

Draw in the picture frame what a perfect day at school would look like for you.

What would you do?
Who would you see?
How would you feel?

Activity 6.5

Morning Routine

Define the morning routine as a checklist you can go through. Being organised reduces stress and provides structure for younger children. They need this!

Make a visual timetable of the routine and stick this on the fridge and on the child's bedroom wall.

This might look like:

Get up
Get dressed
Go downstairs
Have breakfast
Check my bag
Clean my teeth and brush my hair
Put on my shoes and jacket
Collect my bag
Walk/drive to school

Activity 6.6

Night-Time Chat Routine

Preparation reduces stress! Sorting what the child might need for the following day's activities is essential; pack these and lay out school clothes so they are ready to go.

Once the child has bathed, climbed into bed and had a story, take some time to focus on how the child is feeling and to address any anxieties, so that they can go to sleep feeling safe and happy.

Chat routines are great! Use the following to prompt your thinking:

- What made you feel okay today?
- Was there anything you were worried about?
- Let's see if we can work it out . . .
- Now let's think about the best bits . . .
- I can write down three good things about today for you . . .
- Think about these three good things and try to dream about them now when you go to sleep.
- Think about three things you can do tomorrow to make others have a happy day – try to think about these and plan them as you go to sleep.

Activity 6.7

My Pupil Passport

Help the child to design their own 'Pupil Passport' by getting a photo and sticking this to the front of a folded A4 piece of card. Then record their name and date of birth and name of their class teacher on the front.

Next, record essential information that might be helpful for teacher in the school to know.

The following simple headings may be useful:

I work and feel BEST when . . .

1 ________________________

2 ________________________

3 ________________________

4 ________________________

5 ________________________

Things I find DIFFICULT . . .

1 ________________________

2 ________________________

3 ________________________

4 ________________________

5 ________________________

Things you can do to HELP . . .

1 ________________________

2 ________________________

3 ________________________

4 ________________________

5 ________________________

Activity 6.8

Back-to-School Social Stories

Social stories can help all children to transition more effectively and reduce anxieties around the whole process of going to a new school or returning to school after time away.

Write an illustrated social story with the child, using one sentence and one picture per page. Make it personal by using their own words to describe the facts of the process.

Try these ideas:

- Soon I am going to be going to a new school.
- Before I start there, I am going to visit the school.
- On my visit I will get to meet my new teacher and the other children.
- I will also be able to look around the school and see where my classroom is.
- This will help me get ready for when I come to my new school.
- I might have to wear a new uniform for my new school.
- I am going to go to my new school on a bus.
- I am going to go to my new school in a car.
- I am going to be able to walk to my new school.
- Today I am starting my new school.
- My new teacher is excited to have me in their class.
- There are lots of children in the class who will help me in my new school.
- I can introduce myself to the other children and make new friends.
- I can still be friends with the children in my old school too.
- Starting a new school is scary and it's ok for me to get scared.
- If I get scared, I can tell my teacher and they will help me

Activity 6.9

My Safety Rules

Think about what makes us feel safe at school and at home. Discuss your ideas with the child and record safety rules for home and for school. Make up a chart.

Think about how the rules for home and school might be different or similar.

My Safety Rules

HOME	SCHOOL

Activity 6.10

My Hopes & Dreams Wall

Work with the child to create a large poster depicting a wall that represents their 'hopes and dreams' for their new school.

'Build' the wall brick by brick, drawing each hope or dream as an individual brick and labelling it. Y ou might include 'bricks' such as those below.

It will be fun

I will feel happy

I will be safe

I will do exciting things

We will have toys

I will make good friends

My teachers will be fun

We will have games

We will learn great things

Appendices

Appendix 1

Helpful Websites

Action for Children
actionforchildren.org.uk
Charity supporting children, young people and their families across England

Anxiety UK
anxietyuk.org.uk
03444 775 774 (helpline); 07537 416 905 (text)
Advice and support for people living with anxiety

Beat
beateatingdisorders.co.uk
0808 801 0711 (youthline); 0808 801 0811 (studentline)
Under 18s helpline, webchat and online support groups for people with eating disorders, such as anorexia and bulimia

Childline
childline.org.uk
0800 1111
Support for children and young people in the UK, including a free 24-hour helpline

Hope Again
hopeagain.org.uk
0808 808 1677
Support for young people when someone dies

Kooth
kooth.com
Counsellors available until 10pm every day. Free, safe and anonymous online counselling for young people

Me and My Mind
meandmymind.nhs.uk
Advice and support for young people struggling with unusual experiences, such as hearing voices

Mencap
mencap.org.uk
0808 808 1111
Information and advice for people with a learning disability, families and carers

National Society for the Prevention of Cruelty to Children (NSPCC)
nspcc.org.uk
0800 800 5000; 0800 1111 (18 or under)
Support for children and anyone worried about a child.

OCD Youth
ocdyouth.org
Youth support for young people with obsessive-compulsive disorder (OCD)

On My Mind
annafreud.org/on-my-mind
Information for young people to make informed choices about their mental health and wellbeing

Samaritans
samaritans.org
116 123; jo@samaritans.org
Freepost RSRB-KKBY-CYJK, PO Box 90 90, Stirling FK8 2SA
24-hour emotional support for anyone who needs to talk

The Mix
themix.org.uk
0808 808 4994; 85258 (crisis messenger service, Text THEMIX)
Support and advice for under 25s, including webchat

YoungMinds
youngminds.org.uk
0808 802 5544 (parents helpline); 85258 (crisis messenger service, text YM)
Committed to improving the mental health of babies, children and young people, including support for parents and carers

Appendix 2
Mindfulness Information

What is Mindfulness?

> *Mindfulness can be characterised as our innate ability to be fully present in the moment – to focus on where we are and what we are doing without allowing other, intrusive thoughts, worries, or fears to permeate our minds. When we are practising Mindfulness, we are impartial and non-judgmental of what is happening around us, and when our minds wander, we redirect our thoughts back to the present moment.*
>
> ***Rae et al., 2017***

The benefits of Mindfulness

Sensory Awareness Practising Mindfulness nurtures the capacity to bring our sensory experience into our consciousness. This enables us to create the space to simply stop and 'be', experiencing the moment in all its fullness. Being able to be in the moment and appreciate the positive sensory experiences that we have is not simply enjoyable, it also elicits positive emotions that feed into overall wellbeing. Recurrently experiencing positive emotions simultaneously broadens our sensory awareness, helping build psychological and emotional resilience overall.

Cognitive Control The goal of Mindfulness is not to simply eliminate the mind of all thoughts and feelings, but to anchor oneself to what you are currently experiencing in the sensory world. The idea is to allow thoughts to enter the mind quite freely and to simply note these in a non-judgemental and unanalytical manner. This is particularly useful in terms of managing busy minds that are continually barraged with thoughts – Mindfulness enables us to create distance between the thoughts that we have and our cognitive reactions to them. We can have a thought without having to act upon it. We can treat it just simply as a thought.

Emotional Regulation It is extremely easy to become overwhelmed by intrusive emotional thoughts. These very often reflect uncomfortable situations which caused us to feel angry, embarrassed or stressed. Mindfulness encourages a more de-centred perspective on such feelings. Emotions can be acknowledged and allowed to pass. If we just recognise the feelings, then we provide ourselves with the opportunity to choose how to respond to them rather than reacting automatically, engaging in unconscious patterns of automatic negative thinking.

Acceptance Treating our thoughts in this non-judgemental and more detached manner is also hugely positive in terms of accepting our thoughts and feelings. This is particularly important as it encourages us to be more tolerant and kinder to ourselves. We do not need to beat ourselves up for having negative or intrusive thoughts or feelings; we simply must accept them and know that we need to learn to be kinder to ourselves in both the short and longer terms.

Attention Regulation Given the fact that Mindfulness does not demand that we clear our minds of all thoughts and feelings, but rather allow them to pass by and be noted, this in effect provides us with training in how to regulate and direct at will our attention.

Why teaching Mindfulness to children is important

Sadly, for many of today's children, there is little opportunity to experience the wonderful world of boredom. They do not have the space to switch off, tune the world out, and find their inner creativity. The rise in mental health challenges like anxiety and depression are now thought to be linked to this hyper-vigilance and more complex social context. It is also clearly currently linked to the ongoing anxiety children and young people are experiencing as they navigate this global pandemic.

It is therefore a real positive that more and more teachers are starting to incorporate Mindfulness into their classroom curriculums, and the benefits have been staggering. Teaching Mindfulness to children can:

- decrease feelings of stress and anxiety
- improve focus and concentration
- help with impulsivity
- improve self-regulation
- develop empathy
- reduce aggression
- improve sleep

Investigating why, how and when to use Mindfulness is therefore immensely helpful for both professionals and parents/carers who are seeking to support children and young people currently.

Six tips for teaching Mindfulness to children

1 **Practise Mindfulness yourself.** Before we can successfully teach anything to our children, we need to have a working understanding of the concept ourselves. Take the time to learn about Mindfulness and how to practise it, since children learn by example, and the more you demonstrate the positive effects Mindfulness has on you and your wellbeing, the more interested and open the children will be to trying it for themselves.

2 **Get the children involved.** As with most activities, the more involved children are, the better. Set aside some time to explain what Mindfulness is and why it is important, and then make a 'Mindfulness Calendar' that outlines which days you are going to try different exercises and activities, and take the time to evaluate them all to decide which ones you all enjoy and would like to try again.

3 **Start small.** Remember that Mindfulness does not need to be a long and elaborate affair, and you are most likely to maintain their interest in practising together if you start small.

4 **Make it a habit.** Allocate time each day to practise Mindfulness together, and make sure to choose a time that works best for you all – first thing in the morning, after lunch, and so on – and then make it a habit. The more consistent you are the more benefits you will see.

5 **Get moving.** Contrary to popular belief, Mindfulness activities are not all about sitting quietly with your eyes closed while meditating. There are lots of Mindfulness exercises for children that involve movement, (Rae et al 2017) and if your children initially struggle to sit still, these may be a better option for them.

6 **Be patient.** And do not expect a miracle. Teaching Mindfulness to children can be extremely beneficial, but remember that change takes time and it is unlikely that you will see an overnight transformation. As with most things, consistency is key.

Appendix 3

Stress, Anxiety Disorder & Depression Information

Stress

Defining stress is quite a difficult and complex process given that it means different things to different people (in a similar vein as happiness, failure or success). Even though stress is a normal part of everyday life, too much stress makes young people become anxious, exhausted, tired and unable to function appropriately, both inside and outside school.

All of us have an optimum stress level, which allows us to function effectively and efficiently in our daily lives – what is vital is that we learn how to recognise our own stress levels and develop coping strategies when we are experiencing higher levels of stress. This will enable us to maintain a healthy balance of tension, growth, rest and self-nurturing. We need to be able to focus and build up reactions that reduce stress alongside understanding, acknowledging and coping effectively with the sources of our individual stresses.

Children who are experiencing higher levels of stress may exhibit the following behaviours:

- More aggressive or withdrawn behaviour
- Feeling tearful
- Eating disorders
- Self-harming behaviours
- School-attendance problems
- Need for attention
- Dropping performance
- Lying
- Heightened aggression

As well as the obvious stressors that occur in school, children may face stressors outside school, such as poverty, family disharmony, bereavement, abuse and a change of home or school.

Anxiety disorders

When the anxiety experienced by a child starts to affect their general functioning, they may not just be feeling stressed – they may be suffering from an **anxiety disorder**.

Anxiety can make a child feel scared, panicky, embarrassed or ashamed.

Some of the signs include:

- finding it hard to concentrate
- not sleeping, or waking in the night with bad dreams
- not eating properly
- quickly getting angry or irritable, and being out of control during outbursts
- constantly worrying or having negative thoughts
- feeling tense and fidgety, or using the toilet often
- always crying
- being clingy all the time (when other children are ok)
- complaining of tummy aches and feeling unwell

Younger children may not be able to recognise or articulate why they are feeling this way.

The reason for the anxiety (if there is one) will differ depending on the age of the child. Separation anxiety is common in younger children, whereas older children and teenagers tend to worry more about school performance, relationships or health.

Anxiety disorders are considered serious mental health problems and are one of the most common types of mental health concerns for children and young people. Anxiety disorders are so common that one-in-four people will experience one or more anxiety disorders during their lifetime. The anxiety disorders include:

- **Generalised Anxiety Disorder (GAD)** Excessive and persistent anxiety about events and activities related to work, study, health, finances, family issues or other general concerns. People who have GAD have difficulty controlling worry, and the associated physical and emotional symptoms such as restlessness, fatigue, difficulties in concentrating, muscle tension and sleep disturbance. GAD affects approximately 5 per cent of people at some point in their lives

- **Panic Attacks & Panic Disorder** Panic attacks include multiple physical and cognitive anxiety symptoms in the absence of an external threat. A panic attack can include shortness of breath, accelerated heart rate, trembling, sweating, dizziness, and fear of going crazy or dying. Fear of panic attacks in public places may lead to agoraphobia.

- **Obsessive Compulsive Disorder (OCD)** OCD is recurrent and persistent thoughts, impulses or images that are intrusive and unwanted (obsessions), and repetitive and ritualistic behaviours or mental acts that are time consuming and distressing (compulsions), for example: fears of contamination or harm to self or others; excessive hand washing, showering, checking, or repeating routine actions. OCD affects about 3 per cent of people at some point in their lives.

- **Post-Traumatic Stress Disorder (PTSD)** PTSD may develop after exposure to a distressing and traumatic event or ongoing traumatic situation. Recurrent thoughts, images and nightmares of the trauma occur, as well as changes in mood. Other symptoms include emotional reactivity, memory and concentration difficulties. Around 8 per cent of people are affected by PTSD at some point in their lives

- **Social Phobia** Anticipatory worry and avoidance of social and performance situations, due to fears of scrutiny and judgment by others, and fear of behaving in a way that is embarrassing or humiliating. Physical anxiety symptoms commonly occur.

- **Specific Phobia(s)** Excessively fear of a particular thing or type of situation. Phobias can start at any age and a person may have more than one phobia. Common phobias include:
  - *Claustrophobia*, or fear of small spaces such as fitting rooms
  - *Zoophobia*, or fear of animals
  - *Acrophobia*, or fear of heights such as flying
  - *Agrophobia*, or fear open spaces or being in situations where escape might be difficult

Depression

Depression is when a child's mood is very low, with no obvious cause. Between the ages of 8 and puberty, around 2 to 4 per cent of children are diagnosed with depression; after puberty it is around 4 to 8 per cent, and it is more common in girls than boys.

Children as young as 3-years-old can also be diagnosed with clinical depression. However, the therapy used to treat depression in teenagers and adults is not appropriate for young children.

One type of therapy, called Parent-Child Interaction Therapy (PCIT), has been shown to help treat disruptive behavioural disorders in young children. In PCIT treatment, parents are taught techniques for successfully interacting with their children. They practice these techniques in controlled situations while being coached by a clinician.

The symptoms of depression are very similar to those in adults:

- Depressed mood most of the day, every day
- Loss of interest or pleasure in activities
- Significant weight loss, when not dieting, or weight gain
- A decrease or increase in appetite
- Frequent insomnia or sleeping too much
- Extreme restlessness or lethargy
- Fatigue or loss of energy
- Feelings of worthlessness or inappropriate guilt
- Diminished ability to think or concentrate
- Recurrent thoughts of death and suicidal thoughts

Children are likely to seem more irritable than sad, and they are more likely to have insomnia than sleep too much. You may notice that the child does not want to do the things they usually enjoy, avoids people, complains they cannot sleep well, and exhibits a change in their eating patterns. They might start being critical about themselves, or say they feel useless. They will not do as well as usual at school, because they cannot concentrate and do not have the energy to finish work.

Some of the symptoms of depression – particularly restlessness and finding it difficult to concentrate – overlap with ADHD, so it makes it harder to see if a child with ADHD has depression. Because ADHD tends to make children underachieve, they can start to feel demoralised. However, depression is more than this. One study showed that children with ADHD, who have difficulty with social relationships, are more likely to suffer depression than those who are having general difficulties at school. Studies suggest up to a third of children with ADHD also have depression, and children who have ADHD are three times as likely to have depression as children who do not. Depression is also more likely to be missed in boys, because the symptoms of ADHD are more obvious than the symptoms of depression. Boys are also more likely to get into fights, cut themselves and steer clear of friends. Depression does not last any longer in a child with ADHD than a child without ADHD.

It is worth talking to a GP about the possibility of depression if you notice:

- The child has stopped doing the things they usually enjoy
- Their personality has changed
- They avoid friends and communicate less with you/significant care givers
- They seem unhappier than usual

Depression can be managed with several treatments:

- Cognitive Behavioural Therapy helps overcome negative thinking. It can also help the child to solve problems, do more things they like, and support them in learning better social skills.

- SSRIs are a type of antidepressant medication. SSRI stands for selective serotonin re-uptake inhibitor. All antidepressants have a delay of at least two weeks before they start to work, and often this delay can be up to six weeks. This early stage of treatment is when any side-effects are at their greatest, so persevering with treatment is important if these effects are tolerable. If the first antidepressant does not suit a particular child, a different one is worth trying. All antidepressants should be started gradually and taken for at least six months. The doctor will advise when the child is ready to come off medication. But antidepressants should be withdrawn slowly, over about six weeks.

In general, depression tends to last for less than nine months. Studies show that after a year, up to 80 per cent of children are better. However, 50 per cent of children with depression are likely to have another depressive episode within two months. Around 10 per cent of children with depression find their condition is persistent.

Appendix 4

Emotion Coaching Information

Emotion Coaching makes use of moments of heightened emotion and behaviour to guide and teach the child or young person about more effective responses. It is this process of empathetic engagement that enables the child to truly 'feel' validated and supported. This engenders a sense of security which, in turn, supports the child to calm down and engage in rational thinking and problem solving.

Porges (2011) highlights how prosody, eye gaze, facial expression and the body language of the adult can convey a sense of calmness and safety. This then allows for the dampening down of the vagus nerve's defensive system, thereby enabling the child to physiologically and psychologically calm down. The approach does not, in any sense, condone inappropriate behaviours, but encourages the child or young person to reflect upon them in a more rational and effective manner – once they have calmed down and are able to participate in the problem-solving process. The latter will generally make use of solution-focused strategies, with an emphasis on developing the child's ability to make use of key tools and frameworks that are age appropriate. Emotion Coaching requires practice, like any other set of skills, but clearly the results merit this level of hard work. Ultimately, it ensures that children and young people can and do effectively regulate their emotions, reduce their negative externalising behaviour and build their levels of resilience (Shortt *et al.*, 2010; Wilson *et al.*, 2012).

The five steps

Gottman and colleagues (1997) identified five steps that Emotion Coaching adults use with children and young people, as follows:

1 **Being aware of the child's emotion**
Adults need to be aware of their own emotions prior to then becoming aware of those being experienced by the child or young person. Being emotionally literate is key here. This kind of emotional awareness involves recognising when you are feeling an emotion, the ability to identify the emotion, and sensitivity to the presence of emotions in others.

2 Recognising emotion as an opportunity for intimacy and teaching

Uncomfortable or negative experiences and emotions can serve as opportunities to empathise, build intimacy/connectivity with children and young people and teach them emotional skills. By acknowledging low-level or low intensity emotions, adults and children practise listening and problem-solving, and this is foundational for effective management of more intense emotions and the behaviours that may directly result.

3 Listening empathically and validating the child's feelings

This is a bit like taking a helicopter view of a situation as it unfolds. An adult needs to watch for physical evidence of a child's emotions and use their imagination to see the situation from the child's perspective, putting themselves in the child's shoes. The words they use then need to reflect back, in a soothing, non-critical manner, what they are seeing and hearing.

4 Helping the child verbally label the emotions

Teaching a vocabulary to label these emotions is essential in this process. Providing the words can help children transform what may be a scary, uncomfortable feeling or experience into something definable with boundaries. This, in turn, helps to normalise emotional experiences.

5 Setting limits while helping the child to problem-solve

This process can have five parts: 1. limit-setting (if appropriate); 2. identifying goals; 3. thinking of possible solutions; 4. evaluating proposed solutions; and 5. helping the child to choose a solution. What is important here is the focus on developing the child's skills and providing them with a key set of tools. This is both respectful and empowering, whilst also ensuring that the child can and does feel safe and boundaried.

Appendix 5

Trauma Recovery Self-Care Tips

This information sheet is designed to support adults who may be experiencing the effects of trauma or heightened levels of anxiety and highlights some essential self-care strategies.

Tip 1: Get moving

Trauma disrupts your body's natural equilibrium, freezing you in a state of hyper-arousal and fear. As well as burning off adrenaline and releasing endorphins, exercise and movement can help to repair your nervous system.

Try to exercise for 30 minutes or more on most days. Or, if it is easier, three 10-minute spurts of exercise per day are just as good.

Exercise that is rhythmic and engages both your arms and legs – such as walking, running, swimming, basketball, or even dancing – works best.

Add a Mindfulness element. Instead of focusing on your thoughts or distracting yourself while you exercise, really focus on your body and how it feels as you move. Notice the sensation of your feet hitting the ground, for example, or the rhythm of your breathing, or the feeling of wind on your skin. Rock climbing, boxing, weight training, or martial arts can make this easier – after all, you need to focus on your body movements during these activities in order to avoid injury.

Tip 2: Do not isolate

Following a trauma, you may want to withdraw from others, but isolation only makes things worse. Connecting to others face to face will help you heal, so try to maintain your relationships and avoid spending too much time alone.

You do not have to talk about the trauma. Connecting with others does not have to involve talking about the trauma. In fact, for some people, that can just make things worse. Comfort comes from feeling engaged and accepted by others.

Ask for support. While you do not have to talk about the trauma itself, it is important that you have someone to share your feelings with face to face, someone who will listen attentively without judging you. Turn to a trusted family member, friend, or counsellor.

Participate in social activities, even if you do not feel like it. Do 'normal' activities with other people, activities that have nothing to do with the traumatic experience.

Reconnect with old friends. If you have retreated from relationships that were once important to you, make the effort to reconnect.

Join a support group. Connecting with others who are facing the same problems can help reduce your sense of isolation and hearing how others cope can help inspire you in your own recovery.

Volunteer. As well as helping others, volunteering can be a great way to challenge the sense of helplessness that often accompanies trauma. Remind yourself of your strengths and reclaim your sense of power by helping others.

Make new friends. If you live alone or far from family and friends, it's important to reach out and make new friends. Take a class or join a club to meet people with similar interests, connect to an alumni association, or reach out to neighbours or work colleagues.

If connecting to others is difficult . . . Many people who have experienced trauma feel disconnected, withdrawn and find it difficult to connect with other people. If that describes you, there are some actions you can take before you next meet with a friend:

- **Exercise or move.** Jump up and down, swing your arms and legs, or just flail around. Your head will feel clearer and you will find it easier to connect.

- **Vocal toning.** As strange as it sounds, vocal toning is a great way to open up to social engagement. Sit up straight and simply make 'mmmm' sounds. Change the pitch and volume until you experience a pleasant vibration in your face.

Self-regulate your nervous system

No matter how agitated, anxious, or out of control you feel, it is important to know that you can change your arousal system and calm yourself. Not only will it help relieve the anxiety associated with trauma, but it will also engender a greater sense of control.

Mindful breathing. If you are feeling disoriented, confused, or upset, practising mindful breathing is a quick way to calm yourself. Simply take 60 breaths, focusing your attention on each 'out' breath.

Sensory input. Does a specific sight, smell or taste quickly make you feel calm? Or maybe petting an animal or listening to music works to quickly soothe you? Everyone responds to sensory input a little differently, so experiment with different quick stress relief techniques to find what works best for you.

Staying grounded. To feel in the present and more grounded, sit on a chair. Feel your feet on the ground and your back against the chair. Look around you and pick six objects that have red or blue in them. Notice how your breathing gets deeper and calmer.

Allow yourself to feel what you feel when you feel it. Acknowledge your feelings about the trauma as they arise and accept them.

Tip 4: Take care of your health

It is true: having a healthy body can increase your ability to cope with the stress of trauma.

Get plenty of sleep. After a traumatic experience, worry or fear may disturb your sleep patterns. But a lack of quality sleep can exacerbate your trauma symptoms and make it harder to maintain your emotional balance. Go to sleep and get up at the same time each day and aim for seven to nine hours of sleep each night.

Avoid alcohol and drugs. Their use can worsen your trauma symptoms and increase feelings of depression, anxiety, and isolation.

Eat a well-balanced diet. Eating small, well-balanced meals throughout the day will help you keep your energy up and minimise mood swings. Avoid sugary and fried foods and eat plenty of omega-3 fats – such as salmon, walnuts, soybeans, and flaxseeds – to give your mood a boost.

Reduce stress. Try relaxation techniques such as meditation, yoga, or deep breathing exercises. Schedule time for activities that bring you joy such as your favourite hobbies or creative activities.

Appendix 6
Whole School Recovery

Building schools to foster recovery & heal

Given what we now know about the impact of trauma and the fact that we are all living through a complex and multi-faceted trauma at this time, it is also clear that our schools will need to incorporate therapeutic approaches and in essence 'be therapeutic'. This does not mean that they must take on the role of CAMHS, but it does mean that they need to recognise their own potential to support the healing process and ensure post-traumatic growth.

The school community itself is the medicine in our view. Schools will need to provide the safe and nurturing haven that children need. Ensuring those who are the most vulnerable have the wrap-around care they need will be paramount, but so too will be the need to ensure that **all** in the community feel safe and held. Building resilience does not happen by accident. We need to make it happen.

Supporting children who are volatile, jumpy, nervous, scared, hyper-vigilant or withdrawn, or in survival mode is something we will all need to be aware of and confident in doing. This only happens when we accept the evidence from neuroscience, act on it and ensure that **we** have regulated nervous systems to meet such demands, not becoming overwhelmed and burnt out ourselves.

Creating the healing context

School staff may wish to consider the following ideas in terms of developing a healing context in which children can begin to recover:

- Holding celebrations/memorials to celebrate carers/NHS staff or simply the school community itself. It is important to make use of such opportunities to reinforce the power and resilience of the community as a whole and to ensure that everyone feels held and safe. Remember that we can all find meaning and gain knowledge within a communal crisis, and allowing this to happen gives a powerful message to children that we are not alone in this – genuinely. This is particularly important when many of us will have felt very alone and isolated during the lockdown process, without access to this kind of communal support.

- Reinforce the importance of social buffering (Kikusui *et al.*, 2006), whereby social contact appears to have an incredibly positive influence on the psychological and the physiological aspects of social animals, including us human beings. Relationships need to be the centre of all we do. Ensuring that we connect with those who find it the hardest to connect – both children and adults – will be crucial. In simple terms – kindness will need to rule! Keeping lines of honest communication open and sharing our experiences and feelings will be important for all of us in order to feel contained and to provide this buffering for the most vulnerable.

- Flexibility will also be needed. Some will require more support and more specialised input. We need to make sure that assessment processes and identification tools are used across the school to identify those most at risk and to act at the outset to provide the support that they may need. Many will find getting back to school an emotional trauma in itself, so ensuring that staff are aware of how to manage issues such as school phobia and how to support on an individual and wider basis will also be necessary. Flexibility around gradual attendance and engagement for some children will need to be part of this approach, alongside individualised opportunities to engage in self-regulation. Children will not learn without this and trying to push them into academic learning and larger social contexts when they are unable to cope carries the risk of reinforcing and reliving their trauma. Gradual desensitisation to their fears and getting back to routines and structures will be the way forward.

- Listening authentically and with empathy needs to permeate all we do. Children may feel freighted and overwhelmed by leaving home and going into a social context – however well distanced – given the reinforcement they had received over months regarding the dangers of contracting the virus. This is the essential therapeutic approach. It is healing in itself – to talk, to feel heard and to feel safe. We need to provide time for this, as and when needed. This does not equate to taking on the role of the therapist, but does mean that we can *all* be more therapeutic in our interactions. In this way, we make pain tolerable and not toxic.

- Reinforcing safety rules, boundaries and consistent approaches will help to reduce toxic stress. New rules around social distancing need to be framed as 'dos' rather than 'don'ts', as this helps to reduce anxiety by framing the rules as positive and protective of ourselves and each other. Order, calm and reassurance need to be paramount.

- Giving time to reflect on what we value is also important, given that most of us will have spent some time doing just that during these stressful times. We may well have come to a new realisation as to what really matters, what we value and what is essential and important to us in our lives. Children need to talk about this too. What is it they want now from their school community, and how can it be better, more empathic, more inclusive, kinder? This is something to celebrate and hold on to – our children's resourcefulness and vision. **We are creating a 'new normal', so perhaps this is our chance to make it better than the old one.**

Appendix 7

A Recovery Plan to Support School Staff and Carers as Children Return to School

Recovery and rebuilding our connections are now essential and building and **maintaining emotional wellbeing** must be the *key focus* for all.

Encourage a focus on our *values and strengths* highlighting the positives, what we have learnt, what went well and could work again – give **HOPE**.

Co-regulation is essential so ensure that **ALL** staff and CYP can develop their own *toolbox of strategies* and have the chance to use and develop them daily.

Observe and *acknowledge changes/losses/bereavements* knowing the *grief is unique and not linear* and relationships help us to heal.

Value the staff team and put their wellbeing first remembering that unregulated adults cannot support /nurture unregulated CYP - They need their **CALM** so provide whole school systems/peer support/interventions that work.

Explain that education is a lifelong journey – 'you may have missed bits/feel worried about being behind, but we are here to help you and know how to do it – we all have more than one chance and this is not a race but a journey for us all'

Repair for those who need it is an essential – this does not mean a bespoke therapeutic intervention for all but remembering that *every conversation can be an intervention* – so listen, acknowledge uncertainty, be curious and kind.

Yesterdays are there to be learnt from – we all have worries, fears, concerns and we have all made mistakes – be *solution focused* now identifying what we have learnt, what we can do differently in this new normal and how we can co-create new solutions together.

Plan the welcome for all and reaffirm the routines and safety measures – 'we are here to keep you safe and we can do this together' creating a *shared mission* – **this is a SAFE SPACE for you.**

Learn from their experiences – ***the voice of the child is paramount*** – 'I need help with this, I am worried about this, I can't do this anymore' - NOT 'this is what you need from us adults right now'.

Attachments matter – reaffirm these showing that we care, value, and want to be together – *these relationships can and do ensure post traumatic growth.*

Nurture for all within a *resilient, flexible, and compassionate community* will pave the way for wellbeing, engagement and success in **all** domains so ***let's 'catch up' with 'Real Recovery'*** knowing that we **CAN** do this together.

References

American Psychological Association (APA), 2012, 'Building Your Resilience'. Retrieved 9.8.20. from https://www.apa.org/topics/resilience.

Appleyard Carmody K., Egeland B., van Dulmen M. & Sroufe L.A., 2005, 'When More is Not Better: The role of cumulative risk in child behavior outcomes', Journal of Child Psychology and Psychiatry 46(3), pp235–45.

Borba M., 2003, *Esteem Builders: A K-8 self-esteem curriculum for improving student achievement, behaviour and school climate*, Jalmar Press, San Francisco.

Dodd H., Westbrook J. & Lawrence P., 2020, 'Report One: Findings from 1728 Parents/Carers of 2-4 year olds on Stress, Child Activities, Child Worries & Need for Support', from Co-Space (Covid-19: Supporting Parents & Young Children during Epidemics) Study. Retrieved from on 5.6.20. https://cospaceoxford.org/findings/

Golding K., 2013, Nurturing Attachments Training Resource: Running parenting groups for adoptive parents and foster or kinship carers, Jessica Kingsley, London.

Gottman J., 1997, *Raising an Emotionally Intelligent Child*, Simon & Schuster New York.

Hughes D. & Baylin J., 2013, Brain-Based Parenting: The neuroscience of caregiving for healthy attachment, W.W.Norton, New York.

Kikusui T., Winslow J.T. & Mori Y., 2006, 'Social Buffering: Relief from stress and anxiety', *Philosophical Transactions of the Royal Society of Biological Sciences* 361(1476), pp2215–28. DOI: 10.1098/rstb. 2006.1941.

van der Kolk B., 2003, 'The Neurobiology of Childhood Trauma and Abuse', Child & Adolescent Psychiatric Clinics of North America 12, pp293–317.

OFSTED,2020, *COVID-19 series: briefing on early years*, October 2020

Perry B., 24 April 2020, *9. Managing Transitions: Neurosequential Network Stress & Trauma Series 2020*, Video file, InfoNMN. Retrieved from https://www.youtube.com/watch?v=cA7UbKnM0RM&feature=youtu.be.

Porges S.W., 2011, *The Polyvagal Theory: Neurophysiological foundations of emotions, attachment, communication, and self-regulation*, Norton Series on Interpersonal Neurobiology, W.W. Norton & Co, New York.

Rae T., (2016) *Building Positive Thinking Habits: Increasing self-confidence and resilience in young people through CBT*, Hinton House Publishers, Buckingham.

Rae, T., Walshe, J. & Wood, J., 2017, *The Essential Guide to using Mindfulness with young people* Buckingham: Hinton House Publishers

Rae T., Bunn H. &. Walshe J., 2018, *The Essential Guide to Using Positive Psychology with Children and Young People*, Hinton House Publishers, Buckingham.

Rae T., Such A. & Wood J., 2020, *The Wellbeing Toolkit for Mental Health Leads in Schools: A comprehensive training resource to support emotional wellbeing in education and social care*, Hinton House Publishers, Buckingham.

Rae, T., 2020, *A Toolbox of Wellbeing Helpful strategies and activities for children, teens, their carers and teachers* Buckingham: Hinton House Publishers

Shortt J.W., Stoolmiller M., Smith-Shine J.N., Eddy J.M. & Sheeber L., 2010, 'Maternal Emotion Coaching, Adolescent Anger Regulation, and Siblings' Externalizing Symptoms', *Journal of Child Psychology & Psychiatry* 51.7, pp799–808.

Sroufe A., Egeland B., Carlson E. & Collins A., 2005, *The Development of the Person: The Minnesota study of risk and adaptation from birth to adulthood*, Guildford Press, New York.

Tedeschi R. & Calhoun L., 2004, 'Posttraumatic Growth: Conceptual foundations and empirical evidence', *Psychological Inquiry* 15(1), pp1–18.

Torre J.B. & Lieberman M.D., 2018, 'Putting Feelings into Words: Affect labeling as implicit emotion regulation', *Emotion Review* 10(2), pp116–24.

Wilson K.R., Havighurst S.S. & Harley A.E., 2012, 'Tuning into Kids: An effectiveness trial of a parenting program targeting emotion socialization of preschoolers', *Journal of Family Psychology* 26.1, pp56–65.

Young Minds, 2020, 'Coronavirus: The impact on young people with mental health needs', https://youngminds.org.uk/about-us/reports/coronavirus-impact-on-young-people-with-mental-health-needs/